DOGRA CULTURE

A FRAMEWORK FOR REVIVING ENDANGERED CULTURES AND LANGUAGES GLOBALLY

Deepti Sharma
MBA, BHM, B.Ed, Certified Global Career Counselor (UCLA, USA)
Behavioral Counselor, Samsidh, Bengaluru

Aarti Sharma
M.Sc, M.Ed
Philanthropist & Former Principal, Air Force School, Bidar

Krishna Sharma
Arduino Expert, Researcher & AI Learner
SRM Institute of Science and Technology, Chennai

Shiv Kumar
ME (Automation), MMS, Tropo (USA), Rx (Hungary)
Professor, Model Institute of Engg. & Tech. (Autonomous), Jammu

This book has been published with all efforts taken to make the material error-free after the consent of the author. However, the author and the publisher do not assume and hereby disclaim any liability to any party for any loss, damage, or disruption caused by errors or omissions, whether such errors or omissions result from negligence, accident, or any other cause.

While every effort has been made to avoid any mistake or omission, this publication is being sold on the condition and understanding that neither the author nor the publishers or printers would be liable in any manner to any person by reason of any mistake or omission in this publication or for any action taken or omitted to be taken or advice rendered or accepted on the basis of this work. For any defect in printing or binding the publishers will be liable only to replace the defective copy by another copy of this work then available.

Authors claim that the contents in this book are historical for which different authors have different views. Also information and photographs have been gathered from social media/handouts with a view to project the latest information. As organizations keep updating information on their websites, readers are advised to ascertain the latest from their websites.

Dedicated to

Ishaan and Dashea
for their immense love & affection

And

Rama Sharma
For her consistent support during the complete journey of writing this book

DOGRA CULTURE:
A Framework for Reviving Endangered Cultures and Languages Globally

- To create awareness in the public for the urgent need to retain global peace at all levels.
- To bring up the fact that global peace cannot be achieved if the dominant cultures keep trying to swallow the minor cultures.
- To make the governments and public aware of the endangered cultures at the global level and within India, for which urgent actions are needed for making these safe.
- To make the governments and the public aware of the Dogra culture in India, which was once a flourishing culture but started moving on the declining path. With consistent efforts of the local societies and the government, it bounced back & got revived - a good template for endangered cultures.
- To give the governments and the local public, especially of the countries where cultures are in the endangered list, a template of Dogra culture for reviving all the endangered cultures in the world thus ensuring lasting global peace.

CONTRIBUTIONS GREATLY ACKNOWLEDGED

At the outset we acknowledge and express our gratitude to Senior Citizen SS Club Chowadi, Jammu (India) under the Chairmanship of Dr. Kasturi Lal who motivated us to gather all details of the endangered cultures with special reference to Dogra culture of India.

Thanks are also to Prof. Kul Bhushan Mohtra, Managing Director, Parmeshwari CCC Trust, Jammu whose dedication to revive the unique identity of the Dogras viz. Dogri *Saafa* (turban) motivated the authors who started wearing it during the Dogri functions as well.

Prof. K.S.Chandrasekar, Hon'ble Vice Chancellor, Cluster University of Jammu, who was very prompt in understanding the fear among the Dogra community for their culture to fall into the endangered list. His effective actions in instructing all the colleges under the university to celebrate the events during Dogri Manyata Week 2024 are commendable. The authors are really grateful to him.

Authors are also thankful to Prof. Sanjeev Jain, Vice Chancellor, Central University of Jammu for his prompt action in recognizing Takri, the script for Dogri language, as an extinct script and trying to revive it by opening a Centre for Takri at his University.

The websites of many organizations and other social sites including YouTube, Facebook, Wikipedia etc., have provided great input in compilation of this book. Special thanks to the admins of websites of Indian organizations like Central Institute of Indian Languages, Mysore, University Grants Commission, Indira Gandhi National Tribal

University, Tezpur and Centre for Endangered languages, Tezpur for their contributions for uploading very vital information for use by the society.

The potent websites of the United Nations, UNESCO, the history/linguistic/anthropology departments of many universities, archaeological and tourism departments of many countries/states etc. were very informative and gave an insight into the details of many cultures and languages. The authors are especially indebted to all of them. Our sincere thanks are to various govt. departments of the states in India and organizations at the global, national and regional levels who have shown their concern for endangered languages and provided guidance to the authors by way of posting good material on social media.

The departments of Culture, Tourism, Education, Tribal Affairs, Govt. of Jammu and Kashmir, India have done a lot for most of the endangered cultures. The information made available by them in their pamphlets and advertisements was a good guide for the authors.

How can one miss out help provided by Padma Shri Prof. Lalit Magotra, President, Dogri Sanstha, Jammu for his great inputs on Dogra culture from 18th century onward. His guidance has also been a great source of motivation for the authors.

Finally, we salute the wonderful student fraternity and the staff of Model Institute of Engineering and Technology (Autonomous), Jammu, and Samsidh International School, Bangalore who have been giving ground-based inputs on the subject from time to time.

Deepti Sharma
Aarti Sharma
Krishna Sharma
Shiv Kumar

PREFACE

There are close to 7,000 living languages in the world, and one feels shocked to learn that over 43% of these are in the category of endangered languages. That means cultures associated with endangered languages are going to vanish in a few decades or so and the world may lose all the knowledge held within these cultures.

This fact has been worrying everyone around the globe. All efforts are being made at the United Nations level to create awareness about this fact and save endangered languages. Many countries have already started taking steps to save and preserve endangered languages. Still, the bells have not yet rung in many countries, and they will soon lose a vast treasure of knowledge shortly.

This book has been written to create awareness among all. Section I of the book is devoted to the linguistic scene at the global level. The first two chapters have been devoted to refreshing the finer points like *why the cultural studies be studied*, and how the present culture has evolved starting from *prehistoric ages and ancient civilizations*.

Continent and country wise details of the languages in the endangered list are given in Chapter 3 which also lists the prominent languages that have become extinct in recent years. Chapters 4 and 5 are fully devoted to the initiatives being taken at the levels of UNO, UNESCO, and a few prominent countries like Canada, Brazil, Australia and Italy. Salient actions taken by UNESCO have been covered in these chapters which include declaring 21st February every year as the International Mother Language Day; the Year 2019 as the International Year of Indigenous

Languages, and decade 2022-2032 as the International Decade of the Indigenous languages.

Section II is devoted to the culture of one specific country viz. India which has 192 languages on the endangered list. Starting with the cultural diversity in Chapter 6, the facts of the endangered cultures in the country have been elaborated. The complete linguistic landscape of the country is given here. There are 42 languages that have less than 10,000 speakers left and are critically endangered. These have been highlighted along with the State which is to take action. Other languages which are spoken by 10,000 to 20,000 people and 20,000 to 30,000 people have also been listed so that concerned States take special care of these languages.

Actions taken by the government of India and various social organizations in the civil society are covered in Chapters 8 and 9. Preemptive actions initiated in the States of Chhattisgarh, Orrisa, Sikkim, Andhra Pradesh, Jharkhand etc. have been given to give an idea to other states to take clue from there for saving endangered languages in their states. Special mention has been made of the *Scheme for Protection and Preservation of Endangered Languages* launched by Central Institute of Indian Languages, Mysore for its effective implementation.

Success stories of many cultures which have revived after getting in the endangered list or becoming vulnerable were studied. One such story which impressed the authors is the spectacular revival of Dogra culture in India. The people belonging to this culture are primarily in the states of Jammu & Kashmir and Himachal Pradesh. Maharaja Hari Singh, the ruler of the State of Jammu & Kashmir, was a Dogra king and till his time Dogri was the official language and Dogra culture was at its peak. However, in 1947, the State of Jammu & Kashmir got merged in the Indian Union and Maharaja Hari Singh had to leave the State. The governments which took charge of the State did not pay any heed but rather degraded the Dogri language. It is believed that the population of the Dogras started dwindling after 1947 and it was a general feeling among the masses that the decline of Dogras would lead to their extinction in another few decades if not a century.

That was the time when civil society took prompt action, forced the government to give prominence to their language. Their struggle for over 50 years bore fruits when, in 2003, the language was given national status and included in the Eighth Schedule of the Indian Constitution. Later, in 2020, Dogri was made as one of the official languages of the State.

Chapter 10 gives in brief the Dogra history from medieval ages till 1947 when the state got merged with the Indian Union. Next, Chapter 11 covers the family system prevalent among Dogras, their customs, traditions, fairs and other prominent cultural activities besides the heritage sites, a few of which are already at the verge of eclipse.

The linguistic landscape of the complete State of Jammu and Kashmir is covered in Chapter 12. Detailed analysis of the reasons for the decline of the Dogri language were studied and brought out systematically. Starting with the death of the Takri, the script of Dogri, till its status as on date, has been covered in detail.

How did the language revive and who all participated in its revival are covered in Chapter 13. How did civil society persuade the government to make the Dogri language a national language and finally the official language of the State of J&K, are all covered here. The roles of various organs of the government and civil society are given in detail.

Lastly Section IV lists the reasons as to why the revival of Dogra culture be taken as the template for all those governments and civil societies where there are a number of endangered languages. Actions to be taken by every department of the government as well as the organ of civil society are elaborated.

While writing these chapters, due care has been taken so that the readers can understand the perspective and the actions involved. It is believed that this book will be a great help to the countries which are struggling with endangered languages. Even the countries which are yet to start thinking about endangered languages, the template given in this book would make their job easy.

Hope readers enjoy the book.

Deepti Sharma
Aarti Sharma
Krishna Sharma
Shiv Kumar

CONTENTS

Section I:

ENDANGERED GLOBAL CULTURES AND INITIATIVES TO SAVE THESE

Section starts with a brief on stone age, ancient civilizations and finally covers, in detail, the endangered cultures at the global level. Initiatives being taken at the global levels have also been given.

Chapter 1: Importance of Cultural Studies
Chapter 2: Prehistoric Ages and Ancient Civilizations
Chapter 3: Endangered Global Cultures
Chapter 4: Global Initiatives to Save Cultures and Indigenous People
Chapter 5: National Initiatives to Save Endangered Cultures

IMPORTANCE OF CULTURAL STUDIES

Our rich and varied cultural heritage
has a profound power to help build our nation

– Nelson Mandela

Why Pursue Cultural Studies?

The modern world is buzzing with the advancements in artificial intelligence, robotics, drones etc., so why should one start learning about culture. Most of us are also unaware that the culture that surrounds us has an immense effect on our lives. Our day-to-day life is governed by it and even our overall personality is based on the culture we belong to. The customs, traditions, food choices etc. we follow and even the language we speak are due to the culture we are in. Eating choice of an individual staying in Punjabi culture will be *tandoori* food whereas the one born in Bangali culture may not like lunch if there is no fish in it.

This need to study culture as a separate subject was felt by Mr. Edward B. Tylor, a school dropout, who had to move to various countries for the cure of his tuberculosis. Wherever he went, interacted with people of different societies, he found that each of these regions had a different language, customs, beliefs and ways of living. And if one has to stay in that region, one must know, and if possible, adopt the culture of that region, unfamiliar to many. Only then will one be acceptable and survive in that society.

Nowadays, we live in a multicultural society. Even at our workplace, sometimes, we work in teams, members of which come from different cultural backgrounds. To make the team effective it is mandatory to understand each other's cultural background and not hurt the feelings of anyone due to lack of knowledge of that culture. So, studying culture is important as:

- The society we live in is a multicultural society.
- Everyone expects respect from all the members, even from other cultures.
- The cultural differences must also be understood to avoid causing harm to anyone inadvertently.
- Communication language within a group has to be common.
- There is a need to remain united even though we are from different cultures.
- We need to become more empathetic and should be self-aware.
- Even the indigenous languages do not simply serve as cultural artifacts; rather, they equip the user with invaluable skills and expertise in different fields, from the environment to education, from economy to political life and from family relations to social life.

At the state and national levels, governments take decisions and make policies for the benefit of the people staying in the villages, towns and cities. As the composition of people in each region could be different culturally, the decision must cater for the requirement of people from all cultures staying there otherwise the policy may tend to be discriminatory, causing problems at a later stage.

At the UN level, the aspect of cultural studies has been acknowledged as a key element in achieving Sustainable Development Goals (SDGs). In the next UN Conference, scheduled to be held in Spain in October 2025, around 150 countries are likely to propose the inclusion of "Culture" as one of the Standalone Sustainable Development Goals of the UN post 2030. And hence, this important subject should be studied by all the decision makers in all countries.

In this book, the authors have put in efforts to present the culture of human societies, civilizations, importance of such cultures etc. which are taught as part of the course on *Cultural Studies* at the undergraduate level in the colleges. This course also dwells, in detail, the way social structures are created with reference to their class, race, ethnicity, ideology, philosophy and methods of communication.

The authors caution society and the governments about the disappearance of old cultures at a very fast pace, and if not tackled, the complete heritage of those cultures may become extinct in the near future. They have taken the example of a flourishing Dogra culture in India which at one time became vulnerable. Thanks to the spectacular efforts by various segments of society which have brought it back to the safe zone. The authors have also suggested that the model of revival of Dogra culture should be followed by those cultures which are or feel endangered in the current times.

Common Understanding of the word Culture

The word *Culture* has different meanings in different societies. When anyone talks of *club culture or pub culture*, he refers to the activities of night clubs, the discotheques, listening to music, drinking alcohol or playing recreational games etc. When people talk of the *company culture*, they probably refer to the core values of the company, its mission statement, the tasks the company is doing, the reputation of the company in society, the behavior of seniors towards their juniors etc.

Which culture will we study?

In early ages, human beings always liked to stay together in groups, primarily to have a sense of security as well as affinity with their close relatives. Over the years, each group developed a certain way of living, and started following certain customs, traditions, beliefs etc. They also developed some way of communication among themselves, whether it was by means of some common sign language or oral/written language. These attributes are transmitted from generation to generation and are unique to each culture. In this book, cases have been brought out especially of those cultures which are on the endangered list and are at risk of becoming extinct if no efforts are made to save these. Detailed study has been presented on Dogra culture of India which was once a flourishing culture in this subcontinent but started declining due to certain policies and actions. Its spectacular revival has also been presented in detail.

Definition of Culture

Edward B. Taylor, a 19th century anthropologist, defines culture as "that complex whole which includes knowledge, art, morals, law, custom, and any other capabilities and habits acquired by man as a member of a society." Some other authors describe culture to include language, ideas, beliefs, customs, codes, institutions, tools, techniques, works of art, rituals, and ceremonies and many other unique characteristics. So, culture becomes the identity of an individual as well of that group and members get a feeling of belonging with the culture.

It is to be noted that language is a vital component of a culture. It helps to communicate within the members of a group as well as the means for transmission of culture from one generation to the next generation. When a language dies, that means the culture connected with that language has become extinct.

As per some authors, there are six aspects of a culture, and these are:

- **Learned or Enculturation**: Taught from parent to child or by one member in a culture to another through formal or informal methods.
- **Shared**: Culture is shared socially with the members of the community through social interactions, and the common language.
- **Symbolic**: It is the story we tell ourselves about ourselves.

- **Patterned**: Follows one pattern of values within a culture.
- **Adaptive**: To remain alive, culture adapts itself to all forms of environments and also the good and bad things.
- **Dynamism**: It is dynamic as it responds to socio-economic, technical and political changes.

Definition of Civilization

Civilization is the progressive state of human society, in line with the advanced level of culture and standards. It is a stage of cultural development and is limited to a few societies. Key traits of Civilization are:

- Advanced cities even in ancient civilizations
- Specialized and more skilled workers for growth of cities
- Improved technology to find solutions to primitive problems
- Record keeping and maintenance
- Some governance systems with self-emerged leaders and followers

Difference between Culture and Civilization

After discussing culture, let us see how *civilization* differs from *culture*. A civilization is assumed to be at the advanced level of culture in terms of many parameters. These parameters could be urban development, governance system, technological advancement, social structure, food stability, language development, religious systems, socio-economic factors etc. In terms of differences between a culture and civilization, the following points would be more relevant:

- Culture is developed earlier than civilization.
- There is a considerable variation in the timeline of culture and civilization.
- There are no standards for measuring the strength of a culture, but civilizations have elaborate standards to compare.
- Culture is a part of civilization. In fact, civilization can be thought of as made up of innumerous cultures.

In the next chapter, salient features of some of the ancient civilizations would be presented to make the idea of culture clearer.

Cultural Studies

Culture shapes our understanding about ourselves and the world we share. Cultural Studies is a multidisciplinary field that explores how social structures are created and have value even today. It uses theories and methods from the courses of humanities, anthropology, history, literary studies and social sciences to study the class, ethnicity, gender, race, ideology, nationality and other aspects pertaining to the culture. It also provides us with tools to analyze cultural practices, representations, identities and power.

When and Who Started Cultural Studies as a subject?

Sir Edward Burnett Tylor, an English anthropologist is considered to have started the subject of Cultural Studies and is regarded as the founder of cultural anthropology. After his schooling, he joined his parental business as a clerk. However, at the age of 23, he developed symptoms of tuberculosis and had to move to USA for treatment. He also went to Cuba next year. During his stay at these places, he got in touch with an ethnologist Henry Christy who was moving to Mexico to study remnants of ancient Toltec culture in the Valley of Mexico. His travels had been arduous and at some places dangerous too.

Inquisitiveness of Edward Tylor, to know about customs, beliefs and traditions of locals while travelling and staying in the tribal as well as urban regions of Europe and Americas, gave him immense knowledge about them. When he came back to England, in 1871, he wanted to share his experiences of travel and came up with a book *Primitive Cultures* which depicted the relationship between old and modern cultures. The same year, he was made a Fellow of Royal Society and later in 1875 was awarded the Honorary degree of Doctor of Civil Laws by the University of Oxford. He was given the designation of Professor where he started the department of anthropology. In his book he had defined cultural studies as:

"The studies of a complex whole, which includes knowledge, belief, arts, morals, law, customs and other capabilities and habits acquired by people"

He was a practical man who gained the knowledge of customs and beliefs of various urban as well as the tribal societies during his travels. Other anthropologists expanded this definition and gave the concept of culture to include:

- Learned behaviors and symbols that allow people to live in groups. These include the language that allows all to communicate.
- The primary means by which humans adapt to their environments. It includes the dress they wear, the methodology they adopt to heat up or make their residences cool.
- The way of life is characteristic of a particular group of humans which includes specifics like customs, traditions etc. of a culture.

In his subsequent writings, Tylor developed a theory of *evolutionary relationship* between what he called "primitive" and "modern" cultures and said that these achievements of cultures make a transition from a "savage state" to a "civilized state".

Culture or civilization, taken in its wide ethnographic sense, is that complex whole which includes knowledge, belief, art, morals, law, custom, and any other capabilities and habits acquired by man as a member of society. Most of us are unaware that the culture which surrounds us shapes our lives and thinking and we cannot live without it.

Importance of Cultural Studies for Global Peace

The world of the 21st century is riddled with conflicts and wars among nations and regions. Whether it is Russia versus Ukraine, Israel versus

Gaza, civil war within Sudan or Bangladesh, the world keeps exploring for drastic methods to put to end these conflicts and save humanity from destruction. Humanity can never survive violence and distraction without understanding each other's cultures, civilizations and values. So, the subject of cultural studies comes in handy and persuades them to open dialogues to restore peace.

Once there is a will to understand the culture of the other side, the lines of communication will become open, bringing more chances for redressal of the problems, conflicting issues and misunderstandings.

Besides this, are you aware that many cultures have vanished from this earth in the last century and many more are on the verge of becoming extinct? UNESCO keeps publishing a list of Endangered Languages and Cultures which need to be preserved before these become extinct. Most of the countries have kept provision of billions of dollars in their annual budgets to save and preserve these cultures. Details of the budgetary provisions to be made are provided by experts in cultural studies.

The authors of this book also belong to a culture known as Dogra Culture of India. Once a flourishing culture started declining due to the modernization and lackadaisical attitude of the local government. However, civil society promptly came into action and persuaded the government to recognize the defects in the policies, got the budgetary provisions made and now it is heartening to see the renewed growth of this culture. This is the importance of the course on Cultural Studies which has shown the results on ground.

In the last decade or so, many universities and academic institutions have come up, across the globe, to promote this aspect and bring peace in all the countries. Prominent universities which teach this aspect at the global level are:

a. **UN University for Peace (UPEACE)**: This university was established by the United Nations to provide humanity with an international institution of higher education for peace through the spirit of understanding, tolerance and peaceful existence. It conducts many innovative programmes in education, training and research for peace, focused on human rights, human security, conflict prevention etc. One of its prestigious programmes is an M.A. in Religion, Culture, and Peace Studies, which is designed to provide the knowledge and skills necessary to engage in contexts related to peace and conflict studies that are entangled with aspects of religious and cultural traditions.

Besides above, it also conducts Ph.D programs in Leadership and Sustainable Development through its Centre at Beijing, China. There is another Ph.D program in Leadership in Peace, Governance and Development through its Centre at Somalia.

Headquarter of the university is in San Hose, USA, however, it has its presence in many countries including Somalia, Netherland etc.

b. **AUGP UN University for Global Peace:** This UN University is promoted by the Academy of Universal Global Peace (AUGP) Foundation with headquarters in New Jersey, USA. It is a multi-campus university supported by a panel of Experts and Advisors with one residential campus having centers in many countries with a primary focus on helping scholars carry out doctoral research in Peace and Conflict studies besides other subjects.

The university has a dedicated professional team with a mission of establishing Global Peace & Universal Brotherhood. It has been working for over 30 years.

The AUGP Team is deeply involved in effective Quality Education with Social Services for Social Global Causes & Emerging Global Issues, educating the global civil society, rendering selfless services to all global citizens irrespective of creed, color, religion, culture with absolute indiscriminate, inter-denominational concept.

AUGP was founded by Dr. Madhu Krishan, an Indian born personality who has been awarded with several national and international awards and gold medals for his excellence in selfless profession. He is a recipient of the prestigious awards like "PRIDE OF INDIA" and "Lifetime Achievement Award" from US President Barack Obama in 2016 for his 30 years of dedicated service for humanitarian and sustainable development.

c. **UNESCO Chairs:** UNESCO has established many Chairs that focus on cultural studies, including intangible cultural heritage, cultural policy and the arts. Some of its prominent Chairs are:

   o **UNESCO Chair in Cultural Policy and Cultural Diplomacy:** It focuses on international cooperation and dialogue and is located at Bilgi University.

   o **UNESCO Chair on Translating Cultures:** Its focus is interdisciplinary research in the humanities and sciences inclusive of education and cultural diversity.

   o **UNESCO Chair on Arts, Education and Culture of Peace:** With focus on how arts and cultural education can be used for social cohesion and peace building. It is in Colombia.

Besides this, UNESCO has as many as 80 Chairs on Intangible Cultural Heritage including the following:

- Intangible Cultural Heritage and Comparative Law
- Intangible Cultural Heritage and Sustainable Development
- Intangible Cultural Heritage in Public and Global Governance
- Intangible Cultural Heritage in Formal and Informal Education
- Intangible Cultural Heritage and Traditional Know-How

Having an idea about the global level universities involved in restoring peace through various means including study of the culture of all regions, the future students at the graduate or PG levels who are to pursue the course of Cultural Studies would like to know the placement avenues for them.

Placement Avenues for Students

The students who are studying the subject of Cultural Studies at the graduation, post-graduate or Ph.D levels have many placement avenues.

The ones who have already completed Ph.D or MA in Cultural Studies have following main placement avenues in:

- museums, as Museum Administrator to manage all the activities of the museums and take on all responsibilities.
- films, as film maker to make documentaries on areas of cultural studies
- Cultural Researcher or Cultural Analysts in academics or as a professional
- In art galleries
- Theatres
- Heritage sites
- Cultural Ministry in the governments
- As Assistant Professor or Lecturer in universities, colleges and schools
- Public Relation Officer
- Journalist and Editor
- Curator
- Social worker

One can also work as a freelancer in this field and provide information required by many. However, as on today, the top recruiters for this discipline are:

- National and State museums
- Archeological Survey of India
- Geological Depts. of the States
- Government organizations
- Universities and colleges

Good Institutions for Cultural Studies

To pursue an interest in cultural studies, one can join any college or university teaching the subjects of Arts. Many institutions may not have a separate program such as B.A Cultural Studies or M.A Cultural Studies, but they do teach this course, maybe, as part of some other course like history, anthropology, etc.

Some of the prominent colleges and universities in India where these subjects are taught are:

- Christ University, Bangalore
- St. Xavier's College, Mumbai
- IGNOU, New Delhi
- University of Rajasthan, Jaipur
- University of Lucknow, Lucknow
- Elphinstone College, Mumbai
- University of Lucknow, Lucknow
- Shia PG College, Lucknow
- Lucknow Christian Degree College, Lucknow
- Mudra Takshashila Institute of Design and Architecture, Vadodara
- Anjuman-E-Islam's Anjuman Arts, Science and Commerce College, Bijapur
- DAV PG College, Lucknow
- BR Ambedkar Bihar University (BRABU), Muzaffarpur
- BPHE Society's Ahmednagar College, Ahmednagar

If one plans to study this subject in some good university or college abroad, then the reputed universities, as per the QS ranking in various countries are:

- Harvard University, MA, USA
- University of Cambridge, UK
- University of Oxford, UK
- Stanford University, USA
- University of California, Berkeley, USA
- University of Toronto, Canada
- Sorbonne University, France
- Universidad Nacional Aotunoma de Mexico, Mexico
- University of Amsterdam, Netherland
- Peking University, Beijing, China

After seeing the details about the importance of a culture, civilization and the institutions where students can pursue their career in cultural studies, the next chapter is exclusively devoted to the ancient civilizations starting from the Stone Age period.

Fig 1.1: Logos of Academy of Universal Global Peace and The American University, USA

(Source: Websites of AUGP and The American University)

Fig 1.2: Dr. Madhu Krishan, Founder of Academy of Universal Global Peace, USA
(Source: Website of AUGP)

Chapter 2

PREHISTORIC AGES AND ANCIENT CIVILIZATIONS

A people without the knowledge of their
past, history, origin and culture is like a tree without roots.

– Marcus Garvey,
Founder of Universal Negro Movement Association (UNA)

In the last chapter, we have seen the importance of culture and need to go in for the subject of cultural studies. In this chapter we'll study about the start of human history in this world which is believed to be millions of years ago commencing with the stone age. The oldest indirect evidence of use of stone tools and fossilized animal bones with tool marks was found in the Lower Awash Valley in Ethiopia. It is believed to be 3.4 million years old.

Ages in Human History

Complete human history is characterized in three-age period as:

- Stone Age – prehistoric period
- Bronze Age
- Iron Age

Stone Age: This age is also called the Prehistoric Period, millions of years ago when human beings started the first use of stone tools. As there was no writing system then and no recorded history of this period is available, it is only the use of symbols, marks and images that give us the idea of that period. This period ended when metalworking started sometimes around 10,000 BCE.

The Stone Age is further divided into three distinct periods.

- **Paleolithic Era**: It is the earliest known period which would have started around 2-3 million years ago. People were nomadic and resorted to hunting and food gathering. Very primitive crude stone tools like choppers, axes and scrapers were used during that period.
- **Mesolithic Era**: It is the middle stone age characterized by development of agriculture and rise of permanent settlements. The V-chipped stone tools used by the humans of those times have been found.
- **Neolithic Era**: It is also called the new stone age characterized by domestication of animals and use of polished stone tools and weapons. This period is believed to be between 10,000 BCE to the start of the Bronze Age.

Bronze Age: This was a period characterized by the use of bronze tools and development of complex urban societies as well as the adoption of writing systems in some areas. The innovation of the technique of smelting ore brought the new bronze age. Bronze is made by smelting copper and tin or arsenic.

All ancient civilizations are assumed to be part of the Bronze age which is assumed to be between 3300 BCE to 1200 BCE.

Iron Age 1200-500 BCE: With the collapse of the Bronze Age Civilizations including Hittite Empire in Turkey and Mycenaean Civilization in Greece, the Iron Age began around 1200 BCE in the Mediterranean region and Near East.

The Vedic period in India is believed to be during the Bronze and Iron ages. Its collapse followed with the collapse of Harappan Civilization around 1400 BCE and the start of the Iron Age.

Ancient Civilizations

Before studying ancient civilizations, let us understand from *ab initio* the meaning of the word civilization and how it is different for the current civilization.

Whenever we talk of civilization, it invokes idea of the old civilizations like Greek, Roman or Mesopotamia etc. The word civilization came from the Latin adjective *civil*, a reference to a citizen. Citizens live together as political, social, economic or religious entities and they merge in the interests of the larger community. Over time, the word civilization has come to imply beyond organization – and refers to a particular shared way of thinking about the world as well as a reflection on the world in art, literature, drama and hosts of other cultural activities.

Definition of Civilization

According to the Oxford English dictionary, civilization is defined as "the action or process of civilizing or of being civilized, developed or advanced state of human society".

According to Albert Schweitzern, "It is the sum total of all progress made by man in every sphere of action and from every point of view in so far as the progress helps towards the spiritual perfecting of individuals as they all progress".

So, *civilization* can be seen as the overall development of society whereas *culture*, as seen earlier, is more specific to the customs and traditions that make up society.

Sources Explored

It is very tough to write about the history of past events or civilizations. The study of the archeological sources like the old coins, inscriptions, monuments and excavations give us an idea of past events. Literary sources become more authentic whereas oral sources also provide clues to the events of past years.

The archaeological findings are a major source of knowledge about ancient people. Most of the archaeological work has been done in the last 200 years.

The literary works included chronicles, letters, books, and witness testimonies. These provide information about the fundamentals of an ancient civilization. Old *Sanskrit* manuscripts are a great source of history whereas the writings of two Greek historians, Herodotus and Thucydides, known as "Fathers of History", have also provided details of Greco-Persian wars and Peloponnesian wars. Their historical references go back to 400 to 484 BCE.

Features of Ancient Civilization

As seen, civilization is really about the progress and development made by the humans who started living in a structured way as a society. So, the main features of earlier civilizations could be:

- These are bigger groups of people who stayed together in a structured manner.
- They followed some norms for living, maybe in the form of religious beliefs.
- They built houses in a systematic way to live in. In some civilizations, even the cities were built up to the advanced stages.
- They had developed skills and made some sort of tools to make their work simpler. These could be made from wood, stones, iron or bronze.
- In bigger civilizations, there could be many classes, each with some unique tasks to be performed.
- Agricultural farms had developed with some sort of irrigation system.
- The education system prevailed even in those times. In a few cases, even the literature was developed which can be seen from the inscriptions on the stones or metallic plaques excavated.
- In bigger and advanced civilizations, even the political structure existed, and leaders emerged to keep society intact. Even the record keeping systems had been developed.

Cradle of Civilization

A cradle of civilization is a location and a culture where the civilization was developed independent of other civilizations in other locations. Scholars generally acknowledge that six cradles of civilizations had developed with four in Afro-Eurasia region viz. Mesopotamia, Ancient Egypt, Ancient India and Ancient China. Whereas in the Americas, Caral-Supe civilization along the Peru coast and Olmec civilization of Mexico are believed to be the earliest civilizations.

Early Civilizations

Most of the historians consider the following as the ancient civilizations which flourished over 6000 years ago:

- Mesopotamian Civilization
- Ancient Egypt Civilization
- Indus Valley Civilization
- Chinese Civilization
- Ancient Peruvian Civilization
- Mesoamerican Civilization

As per Indian mythology, the Indian civilization was very advanced even thousands of years ago. It started with *Sat Yug*, then *Treta Yug, Dwapar Yug* and finally *Kalyug. Dwaper Yug* existed around 4,000 BCE whereas *Sat Yug* and *Treta Yug* were much before that. Even though the records in Sanskrit are available, still the international historians do not give much importance to these and go by the excavations and documents which came into their hands.

Transition between Neolithic Period and First Civilization

The first evidence of culture was discovered when the excavations at Ubaid (town in the Mesopotamia region) were carried out during 1991. This culture, though considered part of the neolithic period of prehistory, around 8000 BCE, is assumed to have lasted for around 2000-3000 years.

It is now commonly called Ubaid Period, which was characterized with the emergence of complex societies, development of urban centers, technological advancements, art and craftsmanship. Its main features are painted pottery decorated with geometric figures, animal designs, vessel making, irrigation techniques and reed boats.

Settlements also began to appear all over Egypt during around 6000 BCE. Studies based on genetic, morphological and archaeological data attributed these settlements to migrants from the fertile areas in the Near East arriving in Egypt and North Africa. Excavated site at el'Oqeli is in the Mesopotamia region and also authenticates the same in the period 5400 BCE.

Mesopotamian civilization is believed to have followed the Ubaid Period.

1. Mesopotamian Civilization

This civilization is believed to be the first human civilization center in the world. It came up during the years 4,000 to 3,500 BCE in the region where southwest Asia joins northeast Africa, between two rivers Tigris and Euphrates. The word "Mesopotamia" is formed from the ancient words "meso" meaning between or in the middle and "potamos" meaning rivers. This is the area in modern-day Iraq, Kwait and Syria. Sumerians settled in Southern Iraq and Egyptians in the long narrow strip of the Nile River. Euphrates rivers produced rich fertile soil and a supply of water for irrigation.

Most of the civilizations, including this one, came up around rivers which provided water for irrigation besides being used for transportation where paved roads did not exist.

It was known for its advancement in agriculture, architecture, literacy, mathematics, law and astronomy. The concept of writing was found in the form of pictographs. Development of cities with monumental infrastructure can be seen here. This advancement was made despite near-constant warfare among various groups.

They are known to have developed the base 60 numeric system, which led to the 60-second minute, 60-minute hour and 360-degree circle.

2. Egypt Valley Civilization

This civilization is believed to have come up during the years 4,000 to 3,500 BCE in northeastern Africa along the lower Nile River and its spread is most of the present-day Arab Republic of Egypt. It was divided into four geographical zones:

- **The Delta**: Starting from the present-day city of Cairo and bordered by the Mediterranean Sea to the North.
- **The Western Desert**: It is part of the Libyan Desert, and included valleys, sand dunes, mountains and oases.
- **The Eastern Desert**: Stretched to Sinai Desert and the Red Sea, this zone had more mountains and rocky areas than sand.
- **The Nile Valley**: A river valley in the south, surrounded by tall cliffs.

Set along the fertile Nile River and at one time extending from today's Syria to Sudan, the civilization is most known for its pyramids, tombs and mausoleums and the practice of mummification to prepare corpses for the afterlife.

History's most powerful empires, for over 3000 years, are in the region of ancient Egypt. They had the practice of amassing huge labor to the tune of 1,00,000 men to undertake architectural projects and they assembled great pyramids in around 2600 BCE which is no match to other civilizations.

To design pyramids and other structures, they discovered a measure of length *cubit*, which is roughly the span of the forearm (from elbow to tip of middle figure and =18 inches). They also developed a 24-hour day and 365 days calendar.

They also established the hieroglyphic pictorial writing system, followed by the hieroglyphic system that used ink on papyrus paper. Besides this they developed exquisite sculpture and painting traditions as well in addition to being good at agriculture and medicine.

This civilization came to an end in 332 BCE when it was conquered by Alexander the Great.

3. Indus Valley Civilization

Before the Indus Valley civilization started, the neolithic period sites in the Indian subcontinent were discovered at Bhirrana along Ghaggar-Hakra riverine system in the present-day State of Haryana (India). These indications date back to around 7600 BCE. Other neolithic sites found were at Lahuradewa in the Middle Ganges region and Hjusi near the confluence of Ganges and Yamuna rivers, both around 7000 BCE.

Excavations at Mehrgarh (Pakistan) showed another neolithic period settlements in the period 5500-3300 BCE which blended to the Bronze Period. It is likely that the culture centered around Mehrgarh migrated into the Indus Valley to what we now call the Indus Valley Civilization.

The earliest fortified town in the region is found at Rehman Dheri, dated 4000 BCE in Khyber Pakhtunkhwa close to River Zhob Valley in present-day Pakistan. Other fortified towns found to date are at Amri (3600–3300 BCE), Kot Diji in Sindh, and at Kalibangan (3000 BCE) at the Hakra river.

So finally, the Indus Valley Civilization is believed to have come up along the banks of the Indus River around 3300 BCE ago. It flourished between the period 2600 BCE and 1900 BCE (Mature Indus Valley Civilization). Geographically, it covered the areas mainly in India and Pakistan. However, some of the Indus valley sites have been found in Afghanistan and Turkistan also.

The first city which was excavated was Harappa, in Punjab, Pakistan, so, sometimes it is also called Harappan civilization. Other places where civilization flourished are in Punjab, Sindh, Baluchistan, Rajasthan, Gujarat, Western UP, Sutkagendor (Baluchistan) and Mandu (in Jammu).

Civilization started with village-based culture leaving mostly pottery for archaeologists. Later the emergence of citadels representing centralized authority and increasing urban quality of life. They produced raw material for bead making. Commencement of trade, goods, crops like peas, sesame, seeds, dates and cotton started among settlements. Rearing animals like cows and buffaloes was common.

From 2600 BCE onwards to 1900 BCE, civilization saw earlier settlements to large urban centers, inventing new techniques in metallurgy and producing copper, bronze, lead, tin etc.

It also saw the first known urban sanitation system, well-dug wells for water, creation of drains, major streets, inner courtyards and smaller houses. Also, impressive dockyards, granaries, warehouses, brick platforms and protective walls were excavated. Walls around the city protected the Harappans from floods and may have dissuaded military conflicts.

It started declining around 1900 BCE and disappeared around 1400 BCE when most of the people are believed to have migrated to the east side (modern-day India). This may be due to climate change and that also caused the river Sarswati to dry out.

4. Chinese Civilization

This civilization, flourished during 2000 BCE, originated in the basins of the Hwang Ho (Yello river) and Yangtse rivers and bounded by Himalayas mountains, Gobi Desert and Pacific Ocean. Earliest civilization flourished in isolation from invaders and foreigners for centuries. To stop Mongols from the North, they built barriers, which are believed to be before construction of the Great Wall of China (built during 220 BCE). Some of the specialties of this civilization were:

- First written records found date back to the 4th millennium BCE.
- It was one of the very few civilizations that developed its own writing system.
- Developed the decimal system, abacus and sundial, as well as the printing press which allowed for publication and distribution of the Sun Tzu's *The Art of War*, still relevant more than 2,500 years later.

- In 221 BCE, Qin Shi Huang united China under a single imperial state, standardizing weights, measures, orthography and law.
- Technological advancement can be seen from the availability of bronze vessels of those days.

5. Ancient Peru Civilization

In the prehistoric period, the earliest presence of human beings in Peruvian territory was approximately 12,500 BCE in the Huaca Prieta settlement. Those societies were based on agriculture using techniques such as irrigation and terracing. Camelid husbandry and fishing were also important there.

However, the oldest known complex society in Peru flourished between 3,000 and 1800 BCE along the coast of the Pacific Sea.

Peru served as the cradle of civilization to several cultures, including the Chavin, Paracas, Nazca, Huari, Moche and Inca. Archaeologists have unearthed evidence of metallurgy, ceramics and advanced medical and agricultural practices from within these groups.

This civilization culminated with the Inca Empire which stretched from today's Colombia to Chile and is noted for the Andean city of Machu Picchu with its elaborate urban grid. They used pictures and symbols as they had not developed a writing system then.

6. Ancient Mesoamerica

The term 'Mesoamerica" comes from the Greek word *meso*, which means *middle*. This name refers to the region's location between North and South America i.e. Central America. During the prehistoric period, people were found to be living there even during 18,000 BCE.

Some of the most well-known civilizations of Mesoamerica include the Olmec, Maya, and Aztec. These civilizations developed advanced societies with grand architectural structures, innovative irrigation systems, and complex societal organizations. Civilization at Olmec (in the present-day states of Veracruz and Tabasco in Mexico) is believed to be around 1,200 BCE followed by civilizations at Maya (present day Southern Mexico, Guatemala, Belize, Honduras and El Salvadore), Aztec (present-day Central and Southern Mexico) and other smaller civilizations.

Fertile farmland led to agricultural advances, with corn, beans, vanilla, avocado, peppers, squashes and cotton becoming important crops. Pyramid-style temples, intricate pottery, stone monuments, turquoise jewelry and other fine arts have been uncovered. Scholars believe the Zapotec developed Mesoamerica's first written calendar and writing system, while the Mayans are noted for their advancements in mathematics, hieroglyphics, architecture and astronomy.

Aztecs were known for intensive cultivation, irrigation and wetland reclamation to produce a surplus of agricultural goods like maize. They were also known for the human sacrifice to please their gods, often taking victims from the losing side of the wars. They honored their gods with animal sacrifices, raising statutes, and celebrating festivals.

Olmec is an Aztec word meaning *rubber people* because they traded in rubber throughout Mesoamerica. Olmec are known for the statues they carved, including a 20-ton stone head, quarried and carved to commemorate their rulers.

Their society was highly stratified by class and caste with serfs and slaves at the bottom.

Its decline started with the disappearance of the Olmec mysteriously in the 4th century BCE, and their monuments were systematically destroyed between 400 and 300 BCE. Historians and archaeologists suspect their lands were abandoned due to volcanic activity and/or environmental changes.

Fig 2.1: Stone age hunters making and using stone tools (*Source: sapiens.org*)

Stone Age Structures for staying

Fig 2.2: Stone age structures for living (*Source: en.wikipedia.org*)

Stone Tools of Stone Age

Fig 2.3: Stone tools of Stone Age (*Source: en.wikipedia.org*)

Ancient Civilizations

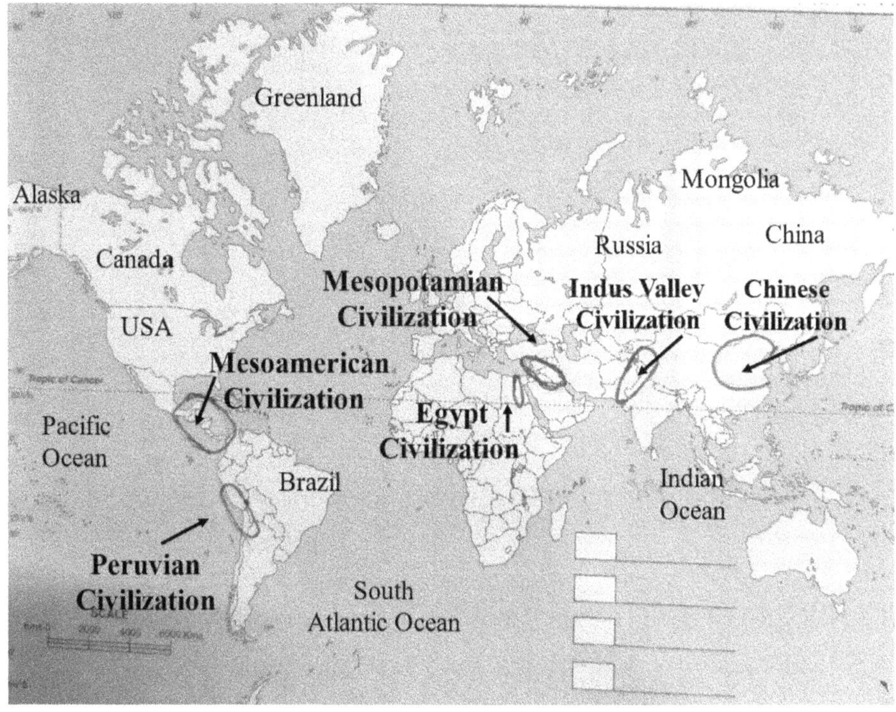

Fig. 2.4: Regions of ancient civilizations

Indus Valley Civilization

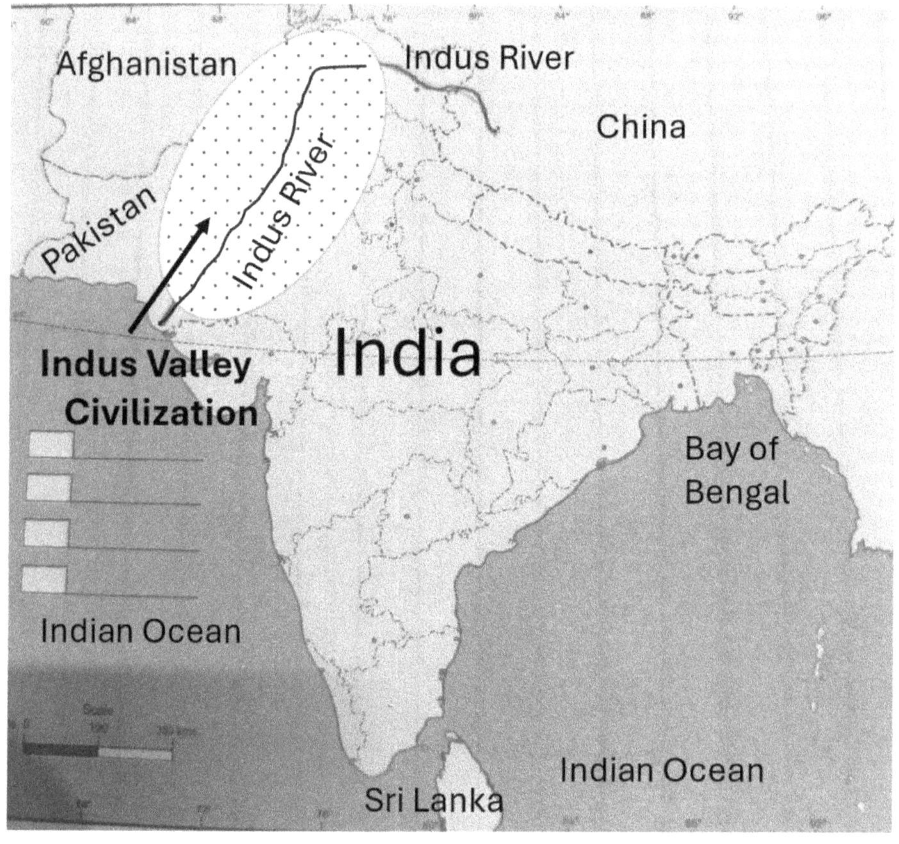

Fig 2.5: Region of Indus Valley civilization

Chapter 3

ENDANGERED GLOBAL CULTURES

Dominant languages and dialects spread widely,
and lead to the gradual extinction of other tongues.
A language, like a species, when once extinct, never reappears.
— Charles Darwin, The Descent of Man, 1871

Global Languages

When a child is born, the first language he/she picks up is the mother tongue, be it a sign language or spoken language. There are tens of thousands of mother tongues in this world, however, the number of recognized languages spoken or written is around 7,000. Some of the languages have unique scripts whereas some languages use the dominant script of that region to write their language. For example, *Devnagri* script in India is used to write Hindi, Sanskrit, Nepali, Dogri, Pali etc.

In one study carried out in 2005, it was revealed that there are 6,912 languages in the world. Around 33% of these are spoken in Asia, 30% in Africa and the balance in other parts of the world. With modernization coming in, there is a global tendency for smaller cultures to adopt more dominant cultures and their languages. So, the number of people practicing smaller cultures declines. And, maybe, in the next few decades or centuries, there will be no one to speak that language and culture may become extinct.

As per a UNO study, only 4% of the languages are spoken by 97% of the world's population. That means there are as many as 96% languages which are spoken by very few percent of people (3% only) and some of these are in the endangered list as of today. Study also reveals that one language dies once every two weeks thus making that culture become extinct and it is estimated that in another 100 years or so, approximately 90% of these languages may become extinct.

> 96% languages in the world are spoken by just 3% people only. Most of these are in the Endangered List today.
> And one language dies every two weeks, making it extinct, thus world losing complete intellectual heritage of that culture.

Levels of Endangerment

Generally, it is felt that the endangered cultures/languages are those cultures/languages which are threatened by extinction. However, it is not true. In Indonesia and many other countries, there are some languages which have tens of thousands of speakers but still these are in the list of endangered cultures because children are no longer learning these and are shifting to using the national language. In contrast, there could be some other communities with just around 1,000 speakers each, but their languages are considered safe because these are the primary languages of those communities and spoken by all the children.

With the help of many countries and organizations, in 2010, UNESCO completed a project on global languages and came out with a document *Atlas of the World's Languages in Danger*. In this document, languages have been classified in 6 degrees of endangerment viz. Extinct, Critically Endangered, Severely Endangered, Definitely Endangered, Vulnerable and Safe based on the number of speakers of a language and its inter-generational transmission rate. The meaning of each category of endangerment language is given at Table 3.1.

Table 3.1: Degrees of endangerment of a language

S.No.	Degree of Endangerment	Intergenerational Language Transmission	Percent as per available figures
1.	Extinct	When no speakers of that language are left	3-4 since 1950
2.	Critically Endangered	Where the youngest speakers are the grandparents and older, and they speak the language partially and infrequently.	10
3.	Severely Endangered	Language is spoken by grandparents and older generations; while the parent generation may understand it, they do not speak to children or among themselves.	9
4.	Definitely Endangered	Children no longer learn the language as their mother tongue in the home.	11
5.	Vulnerable	Most children speak the language, but it may be restricted to certain domains (home etc.).	10
6.	Safe languages	Language is spoken by all generations; intergenerational transmission is uninterrupted	57

Languages already become Extinct

According to the UNESCO Atlas of Languages, there are tens of thousands of mother tongues spoken worldwide. However, the discrete languages recorded by them are 6,700 and 40 percent of which are listed in the category of endangered languages. As brought out earlier, one language, somewhere in the world, disappears every two weeks. A list of a few of the languages which have become extinct during the last few years, in all the continents, is given at Table 3.2 and this list is not exhaustive.

Table 3.2: Prominent languages which became extinct in recent years

Name of Language	Region	Year of Extinction
Tandia, Mawes and Luhu	Asia	2024
Columbia-Moses	Americas	2023
Mednyj Aleut	Russia	2022
Lachoudisch	Europe	2022
Moghol	Asia	2022
Aka-Cari	Asia	2021
Wukchumni	Americas	2021
Bering Aleut	Russia	2021
Tuskarora	Americas	2020
East Sutherland Gaelic	Europe	2020
Ngandi	Australia	2019
Mandan	Americas	2016
Wichita	Americas	2016
Guguthaypan	Australia	2016
Yurok	Americas	2013
Holikachuk	Americas	2012
Kiksht	Americas	2012
Socotra Swahili	Asia	2009
Zumaya	Africa	2006

Endangered Sign Languages

Most study reports mention the endangerment of languages which are spoken and some of which are written too. But the *sign languages* which are there in many parts of the world are often not listed. Examples are the *Adamorobe* sign language of Ghana, *Ban Khor* language of Thailand, sign language of Village Alipur in the State of Karnataka, India etc. Most of these languages are used by small communities like the deaf community and are considered in the endangerment list.

In 1953, the organization *World Federation of the Deaf (WFD)* was formed to focus on the deaf people who use sign languages. It works closely with the United Nations and other UN agencies like ILO, WHO, and is also a member of the International Disability Alliance. It provides advice on *Deaf* issues to many professional groups.

WFD claims that there are 70 million deaf people worldwide. They have gathered data from 130 national deaf organizations who are its members. In its XXI General Assembly in South Korea, it approved the Declaration on the Rights of the Deaf Children. This Declaration contains 10 articles which act as the essential tools for promoting the rights of deaf children.

In the State of Karnataka (India) there is a village *Alipur* which has a population of 25,000 out of which, around 250 people are deaf. As the villagers follow the practice of endogamy, the number of deaf people continues to increase. These deaf people use sign language to communicate among themselves and with the others in the village. Their language has not got any official status and thus the deaf children receive no formal education. However, now the government as well as the *Alipur Unity Society for the Deaf* are helping preserve this language and developing methods to translate their language to English.

In Australia, it is believed that there are around 30,000 deaf people. Their government has declared 23rd September as the International Day of Sign Languages and (23-29) September as an International Week of Deaf People (IWDP). On each day of the week, they conduct programmes primarily to raise awareness among the masses on the importance of sign languages, build relationships with them and promote the use of sign languages in all aspects of life. They also showcase the achievements of deaf people.

Continent wise Endangered Languages

In another study carried out by experts in this field for only 2100 endangered languages in the world, their distribution continent-wise came out to be as under:

- **The Americas**   - 660
- **Europe**   - 136
- **Oceania**   - 625
- **Africa**   - 217
- **Australia**   - 133
- **The Pacific**   - 250

In terms of severity of endangerment, the continents where the numbers are the highest are:

- Most Endangered language   - Africa
- Critically Endangered languages   - Australia
- Maximum Endangered languages   - The Pacific

Severely Affected Countries

As per one study, about half of the approximately 7,000 sign and spoken languages are currently endangered. Other significant features of that study are:

- There are over 7000 living languages as of today.
- 43% of the living languages are in the category of endangered languages which come to over 3,000.
- Only 25 countries account for around 80% of the endangered languages
- Over 1,000 endangered languages are in four countries only and these are Indonesia, Papua New Guinea, Australia and USA.
- 88 million people speak languages that are at risk of extinction.
- About 100 languages may die within a decade or so if no steps are taken to revive these.

As per a study report published recently in *visualcapitalist-cp* who have analyzed 3,078 endangered languages countries wise, top 10 countries with number of languages in the endangered category are:

Indonesia	425
Papua New Guinea	312
Australia	190
United States	180
China	133
Nigeria	128
Mexico	124
India	114
Brazil	107
Cameroon	83

Reasons for Cultural Collapse in Earlier Times

As brought out earlier, a culture becomes endangered when the speakers become less, children stop learning the native language or stop speaking it at home or the elders stop teaching the language to their children. Reasons have been innumerous, however, a few of the prominent reasons which were responsible for the collapse of a culture have been presented below.

- **Natural disasters**
  - **Famine: The Extinction of Maya Culture**

    Famine has been seen as a major cause of the collapse of many cultures. In the absence of food, the inhabitants either abandoned that area or got scattered in search of greener pastures. The eclipse of Maya civilization is one of the glaring examples.

    The Maya civilization was born around 1500 BCE, as the people settled in villages and practiced agriculture. It blossomed between Mexico, Guatemala, and Belize and is also acknowledged as the largest Mesoamerican civilization.

    In the year 900 BCE, the Maya civilization experienced a mysterious decline. A famine brought about by climate change is one of the primary reasons why the entire civilization got wiped out. The people suffered from a shortage of food and because of this, they scattered across different villages. The Maya civilization had great mountains, roads, and cities, which are now swallowed up by Jungles.

  - **Climate Change: Collapse of Indus Valley Civilization**

    The Indus Valley Civilization is often regarded as one of the greatest civilizations of ancient times. Also called the Harappan civilization, the Indus Valley civilization existed thousands of years ago, from 2500 to 1700 BCE. Harappa and Mohenjo Daro were two cities that were part of this civilization which stretched across India, Pakistan, Iran, and Afghanistan and housed five million people.

Its extinction started with the sudden changes in rain patterns caused by climate change. Climate change resulted in drought and famine, which made it difficult for people to grow enough food to cater to the massive population. As a result, they migrated to other places, seeking food and shelter. Civilization disappeared around 3000 years ago.

- o **Spread of Disease: Extinction of The Mississippian Civilization**

  This civilization was in the Collinsville, Illinois region of Southeast America during 700 CE. Cahokia was the largest city, and the people were considered to be great artists, farmers, architects and created art using copper and shells.

  To suit the irrigation needs, the locals diverted a part of the Illinois and Mississippi rivers. They never bothered about the sanitation issues which resulted in diseases and later famine. People had to abandon that land and leave for other places in search of greener and healthier land.

- **Continuous war**: Sometimes the long wars between the groups led to wiping out a culture itself. Example is that of El Salvadore where in 1932, tens of thousands of indigenous peasants and communities belonging to Lenca and *Cacaopera* tribes were massacred by Salvadoran troops, mostly the indigenous peasants in order to stop an uprising. These indigenous communities abandoned their languages to avoid being identified as Indian. So, their language died quickly, and the culture is now completely wiped out.
- **Instant Wars:**
  - o **Passive Assimilation:** When a cultural group is defeated in warfare, the social unit may cease to exist, but its surviving members may quickly integrate themselves into the winning group. Traits of successful groups often spread, and the cultural traits of defeated groups and polities often decline. The defeated people adopt the identity of the dominant group through marriages and/or migration.

- ○ **By Coercion**: In earlier times the slaves captured were brought in the fold of the masters. Comanche from North America are a living example. Women and prisoners were often taken as war trophies and forced to adopt the customs of the winning groups.
- ○ **Voluntary Conversion:** The Christian missionaries who went to remote tribal areas, helped the locals there and brought them in the fold of their culture. Similarly, certain Muslim organizations like Muslim World League also bring non-Muslims into their fold thus making them follow Islamic customs and traditions.

Reasons of Cultural Collapse in Recent times

The cultures where the speakers are less are becoming the victims of the ongoing modernization and are getting wiped out. Main reasons of their suffering in recent times are:

- **Globalization:** The dominance of major languages like English, Spanish, Mandarin, Hindi, Urdu or Persian etc., have marginalized the smaller languages. People seek economic opportunities and better living; they often abandon their native language and adopt the most widely spoken language.
- **National Policies:** Sometimes, a nation makes a few languages mandatory for the whole country, so everyone is supposed to learn that language. Like in Germany, the official language German has pushed smaller dialects like Saterlandic, North Frisian, Yaddish and Bavarian to the list of endangered languages.
- **To avoid discrimination**: Sometimes to avoid discrimination or gain social and economic advantages, the speaker of a language gradually learns the more prestigious language and shuns his/her own language. Slowly, the language dies, making the culture extinct.

Example is that of Coptic language which was once spoken abundantly in Egypt in 7th century vanished due to the rise of Arabic language.

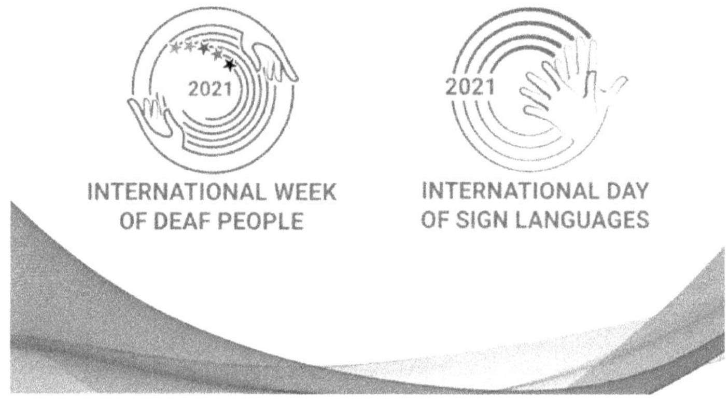

Fig. 3.1: Logo of World Federation of the Deaf and Important Logos

(Source: Website of World Federation of the Deaf)

Poem of Mr. Alitet Nemtushkin,
a Russian poet, who is known for the works
in his native language Evanki

If I forget my native speech,
And the songs that my people sing
What use are my eyes and ears?
What use is my mouth?
If I forget the smell of the earth
And do not serve it well
What use are my hands?
Why am I living in the world?
How can I believe the foolish idea
That my language is weak and poor
If my mother's last words
Were in Evenki?

This poem also finds its place in the
UNESCO's Atlas of Languages

Fig 3.2: Famous poem of Evanki-speaking Alitet Nemtushkin, a Russian Poet

Chapter 4

GLOBAL INITIATIVES TO SAVE CULTURES AND INDIGENOUS PEOPLE

Every two weeks another language disappears forever! Once a
language is lost; humanity loses a part of our rich heritage. Helping
to preserve endangered languages is important to keep traditions alive.

– Robert Alen Silverstein

The importance of cultures and languages has been explained in the previous chapters. Endangered cultures are worried about their survival and the countries are trying to save these. It is a fact that one culture becomes extinct every 15 days, thus the world loses the complete heritage of that culture. Like endangered cultures, the existence of indigenous people is also being threatened in many countries and needs to be saved.

Indigenous People

The indigenous people are those communities/people, who are believed to be the original inhabitants of a region before the arrival of outside settlers. James Anaya, Dean of University of Colorado Boulder Law School, defines indigenous people as "living descendants of pre-invasion inhabitants of lands now dominated by others. They are culturally distinct groups that find themselves engulfed by other settler societies born of forces of empire and conquest".

Number of indigenous people is believed to be 370 million as per UN Permanent Forum on Indigenous Issues. They are spread across 70 countries. However, most of them are neglected segments of society. Their representation in the political system is less and thus they are economically marginalized, have a lack of access to social services and face discrimination.

They have experienced loss of access to lands, territories and natural resources. This has resulted in their extinction in many parts of the world. As they are kept away from the decision-making and policy frameworks of nations in which they live and have been subjected to processes of domination and discrimination, their cultures have been viewed as being inferior, primitive and irrelevant.

Efforts are being made at all levels to help indigenous people, and other endangered cultures to preserve the native and endangered languages so that the cultural wealth of the world could be saved. Efforts being made at the level of the United Nations Organization, various government organizations and private parties have been explained here.

Efforts of the UNESCO

One of the organs of the United Nations Organization (UNO) is UNESCO which looks after the promotion of educational, scientific and cultural aspects for the member countries at the global level. It has a specific mandate in the field of culture, looked after by the UNESCO Culture Sector. They believe that no sustainable development can be achieved without a strong culture component. They have taken up many activities including the following:

- Protection of World Culture and Natural Heritage
- Protection of Intangible Cultural Heritage

In the 1980s, the importance of cultural diversity in the world was felt by UNESCO and it started preparing for it. Its Intangible Cultural

Heritage Section (UNESCO-ICHS) launched a Red Book of "Languages in Danger of Disappearing". Also, in 1997, it undertook a new project "Proclamation of Masterpieces of the Oral and Intangible Heritage of Humanity".

The Intangible Cultural Heritage Section of UNESCO has also started a program "Safeguarding of Endangered Languages". During 30 Nov-2 Dec 2001, another International Conference on Endangered Languages was held in Kyoto as part of the Pacific Rim Project.

In the meantime, the scope of the Red Book of "Languages in Danger of Disappearing" was enhanced to have following four aims:

- To continue gathering information on endangered languages (including their status, the degree of urgency for undertaking research)
- To strengthen research on materials relating to endangered languages for which no such activity had been performed till that date. This would include the language isolates and the languages in imminent danger of extinction.
- To establish worldwide project committees and a network of regional centers.
- To encourage publication of materials and the results of studies on endangered languages.

UNESCO believes that no sustainable development can be achieved without a strong culture component

---

During March 2003, UNESCO also organized an International Expert Meeting on UNESCO Program named "Safeguarding of the Endangered Languages".

Again in 2003 itself, the UNESCO Tashkent Office planned various activities for Uzbekistan. These included capacity building programs, awareness-raising campaigns and motivating societies and NGOs for their greater involvement in safeguarding cultural heritage.

UNESCO's efforts were endorsed by the General Assembly, United Nations and following main proclamations were made:

- Year 2001 as the Year of Dialogue among Civilizations
- 21st February as the International Mother Language Day
- Year 2019 as the International Year of Indigenous Languages
- Decade 2022-2032 as the Decade of the International Languages

Year 2001, the Year of Dialogue among Civilizations

Many cultures vanish due to inter-cultural rivalry. It is important to enhance the understanding of the international community to each other's culture and civilization through active collaboration in the organizations with special reference to the events, conferences and colloquia on the related theme. With this aim, Foundation for Dialogue among Civilizations was formed with the following strategic objectives:

- promoting and facilitating the peaceful resolution of conflicts and disputes
- reconciling tensions between cultures, countries and religions
- promoting and facilitating the much-needed dialogue between Muslim societies and other societies around the world
- contributing to academic research and enriching the wider debate around peace in the world

It planned to fulfil its objective through:

- the organization of diverse cultural, artistic, and scientific events including debates, fora, symposia and seminars designed to encourage exchange between cultures and civilizations in the spirit of the Foundation
- maintenance, and when needed, initiation of regular communication with experts in the field as well as with all other foundations or associations with similar or complementary objectives
- the publication of articles and reports resulting from research carried out by various committees of the Foundation and debates at its workshops

Its observance is believed to have given the following outcomes:

- Helped to sow the seeds of peace to some extent and gave universal acceptance for observance of basic human rights.
- Gave confidence even to smaller cultures that their voice would be heard and accepted.
- Could convey to all that alongside an infinite diversity of cultures, there does exist one humanity. Diversity has to be used as an asset. The use of diversity as a threat is the seed of war.
- Could sow the ideas to some extent that with the absence of dialogue among thinkers, scholars and artists from various cultures and civilizations, the danger of cultural homelessness seemed imminent. Such homelessness would deprive people of solace both in their own culture and the vast horizon of global cultures.
- Member countries could understand the Indian philosophy of respecting all cultures and values and its belief in peaceful coexistence. Regarding religion, it was brought out that religion was personal and based on an individual's relationship with his or her God. Culture was shared. And one should work to ensure the principles of pluralism, solidarity and a sense of shared responsibility.

One of the Outcomes of Observing the Year of Dialogue among Civilizations – 2001

Countries understood the danger of cultural homelessness in case their culture becomes endangered. Such homelessness would deprive people of solace both in their own culture and the vast horizon of global cultures

---

21st February, the International Mother Language Day

Background: In 1948, Pakistan declared Urdu as the sole national language of the country neglecting the aspirations of Bengali-speaking people of East Pakistan. Students at the University of Dhaka, with the support of the general public organized massive rallies against it. On 21st February 1952, Pakistan Police opened fire in which many people died.

After getting independence from West Pakistan, East Pakistan became a separate country with the name Bangladesh. The govt. of Bangladesh had been celebrating 21ˢᵗ Feb as their Mother Language Day and is a declared holiday across the nation.

The Govt. of Bangladesh gave a proposal at UNESCO to declare 21ˢᵗ February as the International Day of Mother Language. The General Conference in UNESCO accepted the proposal in Nov 1999 and proclaimed 21ˢᵗ February of each year as the International Mother Language Day which was later welcomed by the UN General Assembly in 2002 (UN GA, 2002).

The aim is to safeguard linguistic diversity.

Year 2019, the International Year of Indigenous Languages (IYIL 2019)

In 2016, the General Assembly proclaimed 2019 to be the International Year of Indigenous Languages. UNESCO took the lead and developed an action plan for the year. It involved indigenous peoples, member states, the PFII, the Special Rapporteur on the Rights of Indigenous Peoples, the Expert Mechanism on the Rights on Indigenous Peoples and a range of different stakeholders.

The action plan prepared included a list of events, meetings, and conferences which were scheduled under the sponsorship of International Year. It listed the following:

- **Support**: Aim was to focus on improving the everyday use of the indigenous languages and the indigenous knowledge.
- **Access**: With a focus to preserve indigenous languages as well as furthering education, knowledge and information about indigenous people.
- **Promotion**: It aimed for mainstreaming the indigenous knowledge, as well as providing enhanced access and empowerment for indigenous speakers. This objective was planned to be achieved by applying language, communication, and information technologies alongside cultural practices such as games and sports.

Aim of the whole exercise was to promote and protect indigenous languages and improve the lives of those who speak them.

UNESCO worked with governments, indigenous peoples' organizations, researchers and other stakeholders to establish an action plan which sets out the path to achieving the objectives of the International Year.

The action plan prepared also laid out the key measurable objectives, principles and the actions for that year and beyond. So, the main interventions for the three years 2018-2020 were:

- Increasing understanding, reconciliation and international cooperation
- Creating favorable conditions for indigenous knowledge-sharing and dissemination of good practices about indigenous languages
- Integrating indigenous languages into standardization
- Empowerment through capacity-building
- Growth and development through elaboration of new knowledge

An international conference was organized and papers on the following themes were presented:

- Humanitarian affairs, peace-building and national development plans
- Indigenous education and life-long learning
- Indigenous knowledge in science and health
- Gender equality among indigenous people
- Social inclusion and urbanization, ethics and civic engagement
- Cultural heritage and diplomacy
- Technology digital activism, and artificial intelligence for indigenous languages

Decade 2022-2032, the Decade of the International Languages

To promote indigenous languages, United Nations, in their resolution No. A/RES/74/135, proclaimed the period of ten years 2022-2032 as the International Decade of Indigenous Languages (IDIL 2022-2032). It also invited UNESCO to serve as the lead organization for this activity in cooperation with the United Nations Department of Economic and Social Affairs (UNDESA). They were asked to:

- Prepare an elaborate action plan and source of contributions for its implementation.
- Organize participatory and open consultations with member states, indigenous people, academia, institutions and social organizations.
- Establish a Global Task Force to provide strategic direction and oversee the planning, implementation and monitoring progress made in achieving the objectives. It is through this Task Force that the principles of inclusion, openness, participation and multi-stakeholder engagement will be ensured and applied in its work.
- Prepare Global Communication Strategy for IDIL 2022-32.

Aim was to draw attention to the critical loss of Indigenous Languages and the urgent need to preserve, revitalize and promote indigenous languages and to take urgent steps at the national and international levels. It invited its member states to provide adequate funding for this purpose.

Actions done till date are as under:

- **Global Task force**: Following steps have already been taken:
    - Finalization of the Committees under this Task Force
    - Formation of Steering Committee and various other committees
    - Framing of internal rules and Terms of Reference
    - Finalization of names of List of Advisors to the Steering Committee
    - Formation of internal groups and ad hoc groups for monitoring its other activities

- **Global Action Plan: Main points**

    A global action plan has been prepared with thrust on the following points:

    - Listing of frameworks
    - Outlining major actions

- ○ Guiding the implementation
- ○ Monitoring and evaluation of activities for UN-system entities, national governments, Indigenous peoples' organizations, civil society, academia, and the private sector
- ○ Laying stress on the coherent approach and for joint collaborative action on the part of all stakeholders to achieve maximal positive impact and social change with respect to Indigenous languages and those who speak and sign them
- ○ Suggesting ten interlinked themes that enlarge the functional scope of Indigenous languages usage across socio-cultural, economic, environmental, legal and political domains, applying an interdisciplinary approach

- **Regional Action Plans**

  To implement the Global Action Plans, regional plans are also developed by many regional stakeholders. The needs of the region, and availability of resources are seen to set priorities for various plans.

  Finally, it will be the national and institutional plans which will work on the ground and give outputs.

- **National Actions Plans**: Based on the guidelines contained in the Global and Regional Plans, the National action plans have been made. Salient features and work done till date have been explained here.

Inclusion of Culture in UN Sustainable Development Goals

In Mexico, in 1982, UNESCO convened a world conference on cultural policies called MONDIACULT to discuss the culture related policies among various countries. In its conference held in 2022 it recommended that "Culture" be declared as one of the Sustainable Development Goals of the UN.

MONDIACULT is important because it is a decision-making conference that helps shape the world's cultural policies. It has been established that "Culture" does not only contribute to sustainable development but is one of the development's components. It aids in areas like health, education and environment because local customs and traditional knowledge are relevant in promoting health and education and thus must be preserved.

The next MONDIACULT conference will be held at Barcelona, Spain on 29 Sep-01 Oct 2025. In this conference over 150 countries are likely to be present with Ministers of Cultural Affairs from many countries. It will be a decisive moment when "Culture" will be included as one of the Standalone Sustainable Development Goals of the UN post 2030. This decision is bound to give a boost to even the smaller cultures and help in saving these. The cultures which are in the UNESCO's endangered list as of today will definitely be the ones to get the highest priority and funding.

> *It has been established that "Culture" is one of the components of "development" because local customs and traditional knowledge are highly relevant in promoting health, environment and education. Hence, it must be preserved*

National Action Plans

In 2024, a small booklet of 14 pages was issued to all the nations which contains guidelines for preparing national action plans for the International Decade of Indigenous Languages. It guides that the first step in developing the national action plan is to identify the relevant indigenous communities and languages. To work on that, they can consult the fact sheet titled 'Who are the indigenous people?" issued by the UN Permanent Forum on Indigenous Issues (UNPFII).

Process of identification of indigenous communities must be aligned with their priorities, interests and actions. It should be adapted to each country's special social, cultural and linguistic context.

The second step is the establishment of a national coordination mechanism which will facilitate and coordinate the action taken as part of the Decadal Plan. Various institutions, organizations, NGOs, and academia need to be involved to finally get these implemented on ground. In case felt necessary, experts from UNESCO could be taken on the panel.

Institutional Plans

Finally, it is the local institutions who are to implement the national plans. These are designed by public and private bodies, particularly the indigenous people's institutions and organizations. National and institutional resources must be considered to make a workable plan which aligns with the national flavor.

Educational institutions can play a big role. To promote any culture or language, the students from primary and smaller classes must be involved in performing the actual activities. When a child speaks the native language and remains part of the cultural activities, he/she becomes emotionally attached, and then can deliver the maximum. They can also think of the latest technologies like artificial intelligence, machine learning etc. to make the culture simple.

It must be kept in mind that the Indigenous language communities should be consulted during all phases of the development of the Institutional Action Plan.

Example on Preparing a 10 Year Plan

Most of the nations have made their national plans for revitalization of the native cultures and languages. Name of one of such plans, made in USA is:

10-Year National Plan on Native Language Revitalization Roadmap

It has taken over three years to prepare an exhaustive plan for the revitalization of the native languages. Various organizations were consulted, a vast amount of literature was gone through, many roundtable conferences were held and many departments of the government of USA were involved before the plan could be given a final shape. A glimpse on the effort involved month wise is given at Table 4.1

Table 4.1: Month wise activities for preparing and finalizing 10-Year National Plan on National Language Revitalization in USA

Month and Year	Activity
Oct 2021	US Govt. signs executive order No 14049 to prepare the 10-year plan.
Jun 2022	Listening sessions on native languages were conducted.
Sep 2022	Publication of initial consultation and planning framework issued.
June 2023	Review of literature in draft form for the native language revitalization completed.
Sep 2023	Discussions and consultations held with many communities and organizations on the 10-Year National Plan.
Dec 2023	Round table conference and summit held with tribal leaders.
09 Dec 2024	10-Year National Plan on National Language Revitalization released at the White House Tribal Nations Summit by the Departments of Interior, Education and Health & Human Services, USA.

Efforts for Indigenous People

As brought out earlier, indigenous people stay in 70 countries and some of them are facing a threat to their existence. Following are the examples, where there is threat to their population:

a. *The Nuka,* a Cambodian tribe is at risk of extinction due to armed colonists, military conflict and growth of cocoa plantation for cocaine. It is estimated that since 1988, half of *Nukak* have died after they came in contact with the outside world.

b. *The Yanomami* in the Amazon faces threats from illegal mining, malnutrition and disease due to destruction of forests.

c. *The Maasai* in Tanzania has been facing extinction since 2018 when the govt. forced them to leave their homes to make way for trophy hunters.

To protect encroachment on the rights of the indigenous people, various organizations at international level have initiated actions. Some of the salient actions are explained here.

a. **Convention on Indigenous and Tribal Peoples-1989**: It was organized by the International Labour Organization (ILO) with the aim to create awareness for protecting indigenous people from discrimination. It also specified their rights to development, health, customary laws, land territories, resources, employment and education. It covered complete details of the people, country wise, region wise, details of the organizations which conquered or colonized them, their present condition and methodology so that they retain their legal status, social, economic, cultural and political institution.

It also covered details of the "peoples" who are distinguished from indigenous peoples based on their distinct culture, social norms, traditions etc.

b. **UN's Declaration on the Rights of Indigenous People-2007**: It specifies the collective rights of Indigenous peoples, including their rights to self-determination, protection of their cultures, identities, languages, ceremonies, and access to employment, health, education and natural resources. The declaration is not a formal binding treaty on nations but some of its provisions might be considered customary international laws. The declaration has been endorsed by more than 148 member countries. However, on the ground, its provisions have not been consistently implemented.

c. **UN's Permanent Forum on Indigenous Issues (UNPFII)-2000**: This Forum was established on 28 July 2000 by resolution 2000/22 of the UN, with the mandate to deal with indigenous issues related to economic and social development, culture, the environment, education, health and human rights. Every year, this Forum holds a session for discussing relevant issues of Indigenous People.

The latest session was the 23rd session and held at UN Headquarters, New York on 15-26 April 2024. Theme for this session was "Enhancing Indigenous Peoples' right to self-determination in the context of the United Nations Declaration on the Rights of Indigenous Peoples; emphasizing the voices of Indigenous youth".

Declaration of Historical Sites as Heritage Sites

The endangered cultures can also be saved by preserving the heritage infrastructure of vintage years. For this reason, UNESCO has taken the responsibility of declaring heritage sites. This act promotes tourism and acts as a source of livelihood for the locals besides attracting investments from outside. To date 1,223 sites have been included in the World Heritage List thus helping save the cultures in turn.

Besides the efforts of the international organizations, the efforts of the national governments and social organizations play a great role in saving endangered cultures. Some of the success stories have been listed here.

Some Success Stories

Survival of a culture can take many forms. It can be the revival of language, the re-establishment of traditional practices or increased visibility and recognition of cultural identity. Each case is unique. Somewhere the governmental efforts were good and somewhere the local organizations tried hard to revive the culture at the grassroot level. A few of the examples are explained here.

1. **Revival of Hebrew Language**: Over 3000 years ago, Hebrew was a national language of the Holy Land and remained in common use even during the Babylonian exile. After the destruction of the Second Temple, it fell out of common use with the dispersion of the Jews, though it continued to be used as a language of religion for performing rituals etc.

   In the 19th century, Hebrew underwent an unprecedented revival. Eliezer Ben Yehuda started its revival campaign, and many authors and poets joined it thus reviving the almost vanished language. Now since 1948, it has been the official language of Israel and is spoken by millions of people.

2. **Revival of Cornish Language:** It is a language spoken in Cornwall, England. With the spread of Old English, this language started declining and became extinct when the last man John Davey died in 1891.

Efforts to revive Cornish began in the 20th century, with new speakers learning the language and it is now being taught in schools. The language has gained recognition and is used in some public signages and cultural events. UNESCO has also changed its status from Extinct to Critically Endangered Language.

3. **Ainu Culture**: Ainu is an indigenous ethnic group in Northern Japan. They are one of the few ethnic minorities native to Japanese islands. In the 18th century, they were subject to forced assimilation and colonization by the Japanese. People had to leave their land and territories too. They were forced to give away their traditional ways of life such as hunting and fishing. The Ainu language was forbidden in schools. As per one estimate, there were only 300 native Ainu speakers left in 1966.

   Local organizations and govt. helped them to revive. Use of Artificial Intelligence and application of Natural Language Processing lead a pathway for revival of this culture. As per official estimates, the Ainu speaking population has gone to 25,000, however, the unofficial figures peg it to 2,00,000.

4. **Dogra Culture**: This culture flourished in the States of Jammu-Kashmir and Himachal Pradesh, India till 1947. Dogri, the language spoken by Dogras, was the official language of the State of Jammu and Kashmir, the biggest State in India. However, after the independence of India, in 1947, this language got a very rough treatment from the government as well as from the locals and it was feared that the language would die in another 40-50 years or so making the Dogra culture extinct.

   Locals started taking drastic actions at various levels. With the result that at present around 3 million people speak this language, and it has again been made the official language of the State.

Details about Dogra culture and its spectacular comeback have been covered in the later part of this book

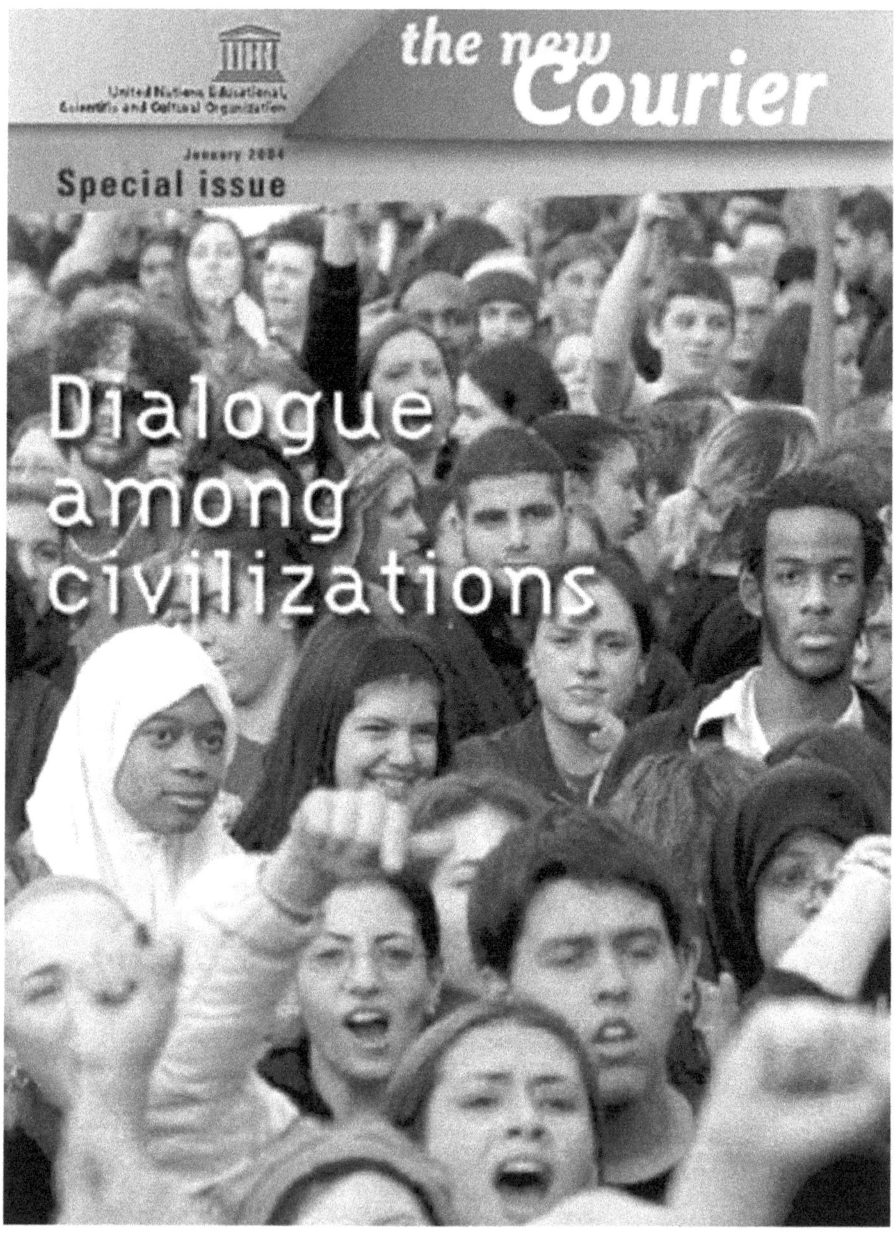

Fig 4.1: Special Issue of UNESCO on Dialogue among Civilizations
(*Source: Website of UNESCO*)

(Source: canada.ca)

(Source: www.arts.gov.au (Australian Govt)

(Source: peacekeeping.un.org)

Source: unesdoc.unesco.org UNESCO Digital Library)

Fig. 4.2: Logos of UN, Canada and Australia on Declaration of International Decade of Indigenous Languages and Mother Language Day
(Source: Govt. websites)

Fig. 4.3: Logo of Declaration of International Mother Tongue Day
(Source: Website of UNESCO Digital Library)

Cultures/Languages Revived

Revival of Cornish language

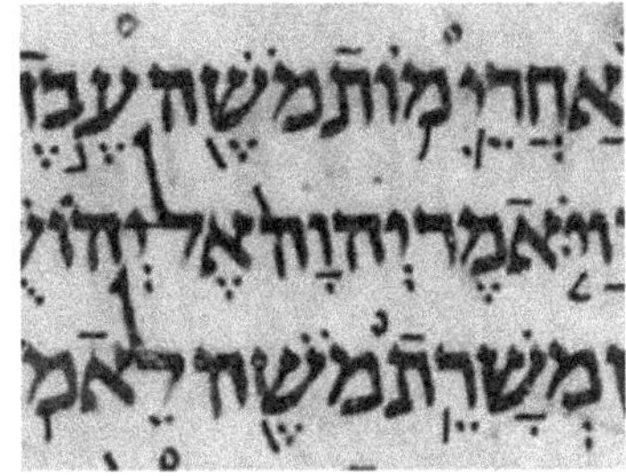

Spectacular revival of Hebrew language

Revival of Ainu culture

Fig 4.4: Logos on revival of various cultures/languages
(Source: Websites of various govts. and wayside boards)

Fig 4.5: National Ainu Museum and Park *Upopoy* opened in Hokkaido Japan, to learn and promote history and culture of the Ainu
(Source: www.japan.go.jp; Govt of Japan)

Chapter 5

NATIONAL INITIATIVES TO SAVE ENDANGERED CULTURES

Modernization and Social pressures are forcing the communities to stop speaking their traditional languages and turn to more dominant languages. National governments must reverse this to preserve unique knowledge.

- Need of the hour

The efforts at the global level to save and preserve the endangered languages have percolated down the chain and many countries have also started doing their best. Works going on in a few countries are explained here.

Canada: Landscape of Indigenous Languages

In Canada, there are many languages which are in the list of endangered languages. Most of these are called the *First Nations Languages*, the languages which were spoken by the indigenous people before arrival of the non-indigenous people. Over 60 languages/dialects are believed to be in the list of critically endangered languages including *Potawatomi, Assiniboine, Bungee* and *Kayuga* which have less than 1,000 speakers left as on date. UNESCO feels that these endangered languages are at risk due to the assimilationist policy of the government.

Latest status of some of the critical languages is as under:

- **Potawatomi:** This language was spoken by people surrounding the Great Lakes region in Michigan. However, with the passage of time English has become the predominant language being spoken in their homes too. As per one estimate only 53 fluent speakers of this language are left now. It is believed that if no efforts are made by the Canadian Government, then this language will become extinct within a decade or so causing the culture to die out along with the history and heritage that has been passed down from previous generations.

- **Upper Tanana Language:** There are five villages viz. Beaver Creek, Scottie Creek, Northway, Nebesna and Tetlin where this language is spoken. However, the dialect of each of these is different in different villages. Currently, only 95 people, above the age of 50, speak this language. Again, this needs to be revived.

Initiatives of the Canadian Govt.

A study report on indigenous languages in Canada revealed that in 2006, 21% indigenous people were conversing in their native language. This figure kept on reducing year over year and in 2011, it dropped to 17% which further went down to 15.6% in 2016.

So, to save these languages, the Canadian govt invested $89.9 million in the budget of 2017, to be used for the next three years for preserving, promoting and revitalizing the Indigenous languages and their cultures.

When UNESCO proclaimed Year 2019 as the International Year of Indigenous Languages, the Canadian govt. acted promptly and in the same year gave accent to Indigenous Languages Act-2019 with the aim to respect and promote all the indigenous languages. The purpose of the Act is multifold with some of the documented provisions as under:

- Support and promote the use of indigenous languages including indigenous sign languages

- Support the efforts of Indigenous people to reclaim, revitalize, maintain and strengthen these including their efforts to:
  - Assess the status of distinct languages.
  - Plan initiatives for restoring and maintaining fluency in these languages.
  - Create technological tools, educational material and permanent audio-visual records.
  - Support their cultural activities.
  - Undertake research on these languages.

- Provide long-term funding for these projects.

Immediately after this, the Canadian government allocated $333.7 million to take on work during the period 2019-2024.

Activities Undertaken in Canada

A few of the activities given below will give the idea of the work being done in Canada for the indigenous languages.

1. **The Iskweu Project:** It is a project that provides support and ensures an adequate response from the institutions when indigenous women go missing or get murdered. This project was created by Na'kuset, ED of the Native Women's Shelter of Montreal.

   Genesis of this project is based on a study report of the years between 2009 and 2021, when it was found that the homicide rates for First Nations, Inuit, Métis women and girls was 6 times higher than their non-Indigenous counterparts. Main reasons behind that were found to be the colonial and patriarchal attitudes towards Indigenous women and girls. Over time, the indigenous people are stripped of their power, thus scaring them within the society itself.

   After activation of this project, the violence against Indigenous women and girls has reduced to a great extent.

2. **Aboriginal Multi-Media Society of Alberta (AMMSA):** Founded in 1983, it is a news and communications society meeting the needs of Indigenous people across Canada from the media angle. It is committed to facilitate the exchange of information reflecting Aboriginal culture to a growing and diverse audience. It aims to provide objective, mature and balanced coverage of news, information and entertainment relevant to Indigenous issues and peoples while maintaining profound respect for the values, principles and traditions of Indigenous peoples.

   AMMSA operates both in English and the indigenous languages. Its motto is:

   "Inform. Impact. Inspire… is what we do. Independent and Indigenous … is who we are."

3. **Canadian Council for Indigenous Business (CCIB):** This Council helps keep Indigenous businesses at the forefront of the Canadian economy and provides opportunities to the Indigenous entrepreneurs to connect with Canada's institutional enterprises with an aim to cultivate shared prosperity. Mission of the Council is:

   "To promote, strengthen and enhance a prosperous Indigenous economy through the fostering of business relationships, opportunities and awareness for all our members".

As of today, it has around 1,300 certified indigenous businesses with over 2,500 members who provide them with programming tools, training, network-building, business awards and research. It keeps them informed about the national and regional events to advance economic reconciliation across the country thus helping the Indigenous entrepreneurs for sustained growth.

Brazil: Landscape of Indigenous Peoples

Brazil, during the 1500s, was inhibited by close to 11 million indigenous people, living in around 2,000 tribes. They used to speak the language of the Tupi-Guarani families. During the 16th century, the Portuguese came here and made it one of their colonies. They created sugarcane plantations along the coastal areas and enslaved many locals to work on their plantations.

It is believed that during the first century of contact with the outsiders, 90% of their population was wiped out due to diseases imported by the colonists. In the following centuries, thousands more died or enslaved in the rubber and sugar cane plantations.

Brazil got independence in 1822 from Portugal. But still the situation was not very rosy. During this period, Brazil witnessed many revolts within the tribes and military dictatorship before it became a democratic country. It is estimated that one tribe became extinct every year over the last century. Taking note of this drop in population of indigenous people, in 1950, Darcy Ribeiro, an eminent senator and anthropologist, predicted that there would be no indigenous people left by the year 1980.

In 1967, a federal prosecutor named Jader Figueiredo published a 7,000-page report cataloguing thousands of atrocities and crimes committed against Indigenous people, ranging from murder to land theft to enslavement. Also, when the Amazon was opened up for development by the military in the 1960s, 1970s and 1980s, a new wave of modernization started. Many hydro-electric dams, cattle ranches, buildings and roads came up. As per one report, the indigenous people lost their lands and dozens of tribes disappeared forever.

Indigenous people play a very vital role in preserving the ecology and conserving biodiversity. They have unrivalled knowledge of their plants and animals and are the best guardians of the natural world.

Besides above, there are over one hundred uncontacted tribes in the world and Brazil is home to a maximum of these. They are not backward or primitive relics of a remote past, but they are our contemporaries and a very vital part of humankind's diversity.

As per one estimate, 1.7 million people in Brazil (0.8% of the population of Brazil) are the Indigenous Peoples, who belong to around 305 tribes.

> As on today, there are over 100 uncontactable tribes in the world. They are indigenous people who avoid contact with outside world.
> Majority of them live in Brazil.

Initiatives of Govt. of Brazil

The Government of Brazil has taken many steps to save the indigenous people and also preserve their culture. Salient initiatives taken by them are as under:

- The Brazilian government has created a separate Ministry for Indigenous Peoples. It has also decided to appoint the indigenous people to government positions. Lately, Joenia Wapichana was appointed as the President of Funai, Brazil's National Agency for Indigenous Affairs.
- The Govt. has provided legal protection to safeguard the interests of the indigenous peoples by making many provisions in its Constitution. Some of these are:
  - The Brazilian constitution now recognizes the rights of Indigenous peoples to live in their traditional territories.
  - The government has taken the responsibility to demarcate the land belonging to indigenous peoples.
  - The government has taken the responsibility for providing bilingual education and health care adapted to Indigenous needs and beliefs.

Besides this, the government has taken many actions to save and preserve culture and languages of the indigenous people, a few of these are:

- **Stopping Illegal Mining in Indigenous Land**: The Federal Police keeps a watch on the illegal entry of the miners in the land designated for the indigenous people. A task force has been set up to end the illegal mining in their areas and very lately, the police started a campaign to remove all the illegal miners from their land.

- **Declaration of New Indigenous Territories**: Recently, in April 2023, Lula da Silva, Brazilian President, formalized demarcation of 13 new Indigenous territories. Now deforestation will stop in these forest areas, which will help in preservation of ecology also.
- The President also promised to work on identification and declaration of more Indigenous territories out of the 261 Indigenous territories claimed by them.

Australia – Landscape of Indigenous Peoples

Indigenous peoples in Australia have distinct groups with unique cultures, languages, and belief systems. It is believed that they are one of the oldest living populations in the world. As per the scientists, the first people who came to Australia were from Asia, possibly around Timor around 50,000 years ago. They were mostly the hunter-gatherers who used to live in groups called bands. Most prominent indigenous people or First Nations Peoples are Aboriginal or Torres Strait Islanders. They are not one group but comprise of hundreds of groups each having its own distinct language, history and cultural traditions.

The population of indigenous peoples was likely to be 300,000-1,000,000 before colonization by Europeans commenced. They were subjected to many diseases and the violent policy of "pacification by force" in the 19th century. Use of tobacco is very prevalent among the population of 15 years and older leading to their health problems and even the premature deaths. By the turn of the century (1901), their population got reduced to around 117,000.

During all these years, they faced social injustice and discriminatory government policies. They are still the socially and economically disadvantaged people of Australia. Even when the Constitution of Australia was drafted in 1901, it considered Aboriginal and Torres

Strait Islander people as a 'dying race' and not worthy of citizenship or humanity. So, they were excluded from discussion about creation of a new nation to be situated on their ancestral land and waters.

As of today, around 24% of the indigenous people still stay in remote areas where the disparity is more pronounced. They get less health benefits, educational and employment opportunities than other Australians.

Australiana Constitution, in 1901, treated Aboriginal peoples differently. They were excluded from the national population count. They gave Commonwealth the power to make laws for all Australians other than Aboriginal people.

However, in 1971, they were included in the Census of Population for the first time and recorded their population as 115,953.

Initiatives by Govt. of Australia

The Govt. of Australia has taken many initiatives to improve the condition of the indigenous peoples and remove the disparity. Sizable funding by the government is improving their living conditions now. The population of indigenous people in 2010 had gone up to 745,000 which is 3% of the population of Australia. Salient initiatives of the government are listed here.

- In 1962, the right of voting was given to the indigenous people by Commonwealth legislation.
- In 1967, the Constitution was amended to include the Aboriginal and Torres Strait Islander peoples to be counted as part of the national population, and for the Commonwealth government to make laws for them.
- In 1992, a high court decision made the Aboriginal and Torres Strait Islander peoples as the First peoples of Australia and the notion of 'terra nullius' (unoccupied land prior to colonization) was removed. However, on ground it is still felt that some discrimination exists for these Aboriginal people.

- **Formation of National Indigenous Australians Agency (NIAA)**: This agency was formed in 2019 with the vision as:

  "Aboriginal and Torres Strait Islander Peoples are heard, recognized and empowered."

  It works in partnership to enable the self-determination and aspirations of First Nations communities. It leads and influences change across government to ensure Aboriginal and Torres Strait Islander peoples have a say in the decisions that affect them. It funds the projects that help the indigenous Australians, including others focused on health, wellbeing, housing and community safety.

- **National Agreement on Closing the Gap:** A commitment by all Australian governments to improve the lives of Indigenous Australians has been made.
- **National Aboriginal and Torres Strait Islander Health Plan**: Under this plan, the policy decisions for health and wellbeing of Indigenous peoples are taken.
- **Indigenous Australians' Health Programme (IAHP)**: Proportionate funds are provided to improve access to health care of all including indigenous peoples.
- **Indigenous Advancement Strategy (IAS):** Promotes jobs and economic opportunities for Indigenous Australians.

Other initiatives include formation of many organizations like Australian Institute of Aboriginal and Torres Strait Islander Studies (AIATSIS), The Lowitja Institute, Australian Indigenous HealthInfoNet, National Native Title Tribunal, Indigenous Land and Sea Corporation etc.

Italy: Landscape of Languages

In Europe, Italy is one of those countries which has a different kind of linguistic diversity landscape. For such a small country, the number of languages are very many which differ from each other in many respects. These languages depict the local traditions, knowledge and history of the regions where these are spoken. As per UNESCO *Atlas of World's Languages in Danger*, the number of languages which are in the Endangered List are 31, and these are at risk of disappearing. Special care is needed for these languages at all levels. Linguistic diversity in Italy is well summarized in the book, *The Dialects of Italy* authored by Maiden and Parry which says:

> *"Italy holds especial treasures for linguists. There is probably no other area in Europe in which such a profusion of linguistic variation is concentrated into so small a geographical area."*

In the earlier Roman Empires, classical Latin was the language spoken. However, during the Renaissance, the Italian thinkers coined a new word "Vulgar Latin" i.e. "corrupted" form of Latin which was easy to use. The languages originated from Vulgar Latin are also called Romance Languages (i.e. Roman Languages).

Currently, the official and most widely spoken language across Italy is Italian and is spoken by 97% of the citizens. Besides this, citizens know other languages also as second language like English, French, Spanish etc. However, almost all the Romance languages spoken in Italy are native to that area. Besides the main language, there are many dialects.

25% people use both the dialects and main Italian languages whereas 12.5% use local dialects only. According to UNESCO, there are 31 endangered languages in Italy. These languages include indigenous Romance languages like Friulian, Venetian, Sicilian, Calabrese, Neapolitan, Friulian etc. Other languages in the endangered list are:

- Germanic Languages
  - Cimbrian
  - Walser
  - M'ocheno
  - Toitschu

- Other Languages
  - Griko

- ○ Calabrian Greek
- ○ Molise Slavic Serbo-Croatian
- ○ Arbereshe Albanian

Majority of the languages in the endangered list have no standardized written form and are just occasionally written. Decline of these started in 1861 when the kingdom of Italy was formed which imposed Italian language on all the citizens. Even in the 1900s, Italian was still a new language to many locals who lived in rural and poor areas. They never considered Italian as their language. As the locals had to shift from their language to Italian, disappearance of these local languages started and that is how these have now come in the category of the Endangered Languages.

Second reason is that of colonization and conquest by powerful groups who forced everyone to adopt their cultural and linguistic practices.

All these endangered languages have at least one of the following commonalities:

- These are primarily spoken and have no written format or script.
- These are spoken in just informal gatherings only.
- These are variants of some other dialects thus creating problems in standardizing these.

Initiatives of Italian Govt.

The government of Italy has started many programmes and taken many initiatives to save and preserve the endangered languages. In addition, some of the communities have also taken up projects to save and preserve these languages. Some of the initiatives taken are:

- **Provision of Official Status**: In 1999, the government accorded official recognition to 12 of the endangered regional and minority languages. Some of these are French, Provençal, Franco-Provençal, German, Ladin, Friulian, Slovene, Sardinian, Catalan, and Albanian.

This recognition will give the same protection to these 12 languages as to other languages. Besides, these linguistic minorities will have local self- governments of their own.

- **Formation of Endangered Languages Alliance (ELA)**: This Alliance has taken up the Italian *Languages Project* that encompasses work on some of the languages and dialects of Italy besides standard Italian. Some of the endangered languages like Sicilian, Neapolitan and Calabrese have also been taken for preservation. These languages are currently spoken by older people who had migrated from USA and their children are immigrants. Presently, these languages are used by poets, artists and other activists.

- **Starting *Sportello Linguistico***: Under this initiative, a linguistic office is opened up to promote and protect the Grecanico language. Other initiatives include *Sportello Linguistico Regionale (SLR) for the Molise* to protect the Arberesche and Croatian linguistic and cultural communities in the Molise region; and *Sportello Linguistico Cimbro dei Sette Comuni* to promote Cimbrian language and culture through courses, meetings and materials.

- **Research on Romagnolo:** A research program for this language has started to ascertain as to how to preserve and revitalize endangered languages like Romagnolo. Also, aspects like the way a language affects the group's identity and culture is being studied.

- **Initiative by University of Southern California (USC)**: This university conducts many *study abroad programs* in Italy in Florence, Milan, Perugia and Rome. While doing research on endangered languages, the undergraduate students at this university conveyed that a language is the fabric of civilization as well as of a family. So, before these endangered languages are forgotten, they would carry out research and find out methods for their safety and preservation.

Under the guidance of Khalil Iskarous, an USC Linguistic expert, in 2018, the students undertook a summer research trip in many areas of Italy. They interacted with the people speaking Ladin, a language spoken by just a few hundred people in Italy's Fass Valley, recorded the conversation and the folklore. They also had a plan to use technology to analyze these audio clippings and create outlines of the language's basic rules for making sentences etc.

Other Countries

Most of the countries are taking cues from the initiatives of UNESCO and started identifying the endangered languages in their own countries. It is believed that these initiatives will help in saving those languages which otherwise would have become extinct in a few decades from now. Let us hope that linguistic diversity will be maintained and the vast treasure of knowledge held within these cultures would not be lost forever.

Fig 5.1: Justin Trudeau, the Canadian Prime Minister, in a reconciliation bid with Indigenous people

Fig 5.2: A TV programme highlighting violence against
Indigenous women and girls in Montreal
(Source: City News)

Fig 5.3: Cacique Raoni, Leader of Indigenous Peoples, with President Lula De
Silva during swearing in ceremony in January 2023.
(Source: Tânia Rego/Agência Brasil)

Fig 5.4: Lula De Silva, the President of Brazil signing Act for demarcation of 13 territories for the Indigenous People
(Source: Mongabay, Brazil)

Fig 5.5: Glimpse of Indigenous people in Australia
(Source: iwgia.org/en/Australia)

Fig 5.6: Trade unions marching in a rally for Aboriginal Peoples during May 1966 demanding full citizenship and education for them in Australia
(Source: espace.library.uq.edu.au)

Fig 5.7: Rally demanding Agreement with the First Nations Peoples in Australia
(Source: atn.ns.au)

Fig 5.8: A roadside board still written in local language in Italy
(Source: quibrescia.it)

Section II:

INDIAN CULTURES AT THE RISK OF EXTINCTION

Cultural diversity in India has been explained in this section before bringing out details of the endangered languages. Extensive initiatives of the Indian government as well as the local society have also been covered in this section.

Chapter 6

CULTURAL DIVERSITY IN INDIA

India's cultural vibrancy and diversity makes us stronger.
It is a matter of great joy to be among people and celebrate aspects of their unique heritage.

– Narendra Modi, Prime Minister of India (2014 till date)

India is home to around 1.40 billion people and accommodates interesting cultural diversity comprising of different languages, religious traditions, geographical regions, ethnicity and festivals. So, Indian culture is a way of life. Being a vast country, the cultural diversity is spread over a large number of major and smaller towns, villages, hilly areas and even in the isolated islands. It is an amalgamation of various traditions, customs, beliefs, rituals, languages and a variety of festivals and fairs.

Cultural Diversity, as defined by O'Reilly is:

> *"A group is diverse if it is composed of individuals who differ on a characteristic on which they base their own social identity".*

Another common definition of diversity pertaining to culture is:

> *"The representation, in one social system of people with distinctly different group affiliations of cultural significance.*

Cultural diversity in India is well contained in the Census Report of 2011, when the population of India was 1.21 billion who speak over 19,569 mother tongues. Each mother tongue signifies a unique culture with its own traditions, customs, food habits and its inherited wealth of knowledge. However, there would have been thousands of other mother tongues which have become extinct due to many reasons as explained in the earlier chapter. But still, these 19,569 mother tongues depict the cultural diversity in the country.

Indian culture is the oldest culture in the world. Even during Bronze era, India had urban civilization, known as Indus Valley Civilization

Indus Valley Civilization

Before going in for the details of the cultural diversity of India, let us have a look at the ancient civilizations in India, popularly called Indus Valley Civilization.

Documented records show that India is the oldest continuous living civilization in the world. DNA studies from the Rakhigarhi excavations in Harayana depicted the Indus valley civilization to have flourished way back around 8,000 BCE. However, the Indian rock art and several rock painting sites in India are estimated to be between about 40,000-1,00,000 years old, uninfluenced architectural designs with prioritized practical functionality. Unlike grand palaces, monuments, or tombs, most structures were large-scale public buildings and spacious houses. This means the Indian civilization goes back to the prehistoric periods.

In an *Evaluation Report of UNESCO* on the excavated shelters at Bhimbetka cave in India, human occupations have been estimated to be around 100,000 BCE to 1,000 CE. This cave is one of the world heritage sites of UNESCO. Some excavated sites at Harappa (Punjab), Mohenjo Daro (Sindh), Rakhigarhi (Haryana), Dholavira (Gujarat), Ganweriwala (Cholistan) depict advanced civilization even around 10,000 years ago.

Indus Valley Civilization was a Bronze Age civilization in the northwestern regions of South Asia. This civilization flourished in the alluvial plains of the Indus River which flows through Pakistan and India. It had developed proper know-how for the best use of land, design of urban environment and proper agricultural system. The Indus cities are noted for their urban planning, technical advancement and stable political process. They are also noted for their baked brick houses, elaborate drainage systems, water supply systems, and clusters of large and non-residential buildings.

The Harappan excavations indicated cities with arterial roads, smaller lanes, big as well as small houses and courtyards having carefully planned drainage systems. The Indus valley civilization is also called the Harappan culture.

Linguistic Diversity

Census of India-2011 is the only recent authenticated report till date which gives details of mother tongues, 19,569 in number, as well as the languages spoken in today's India. 19,569 mother tongues mean that as many unique cultures. Some of these mother tongues are only spoken with no script or method to write these. However, when these were subjected to linguistic scrutiny, edited, scrutinized and clubbed, the number came out as 1,369 *rationalized mother tongues* whereas 1,474 were categorized as *unclassified other mother tongues*. The classified mother tongues which were spoken by more than 10,000 persons and have script for writing gave a figure of 121 languages.

So, the Constitution of India recognizes these 121 languages as the major languages and presents these in two parts. Part A consists of 22 major languages and is called Scheduled Languages whereas Part B, with 99 languages is called Non-Scheduled Languages.

When the country became independent, there were 14 languages as Scheduled Languages. These were Assamese, Bengali, Gujarati, Hindi, Kannada, Kashmiri, Malayalam, Marathi, Oriya, Punjabi, Sanskrit, Tamil, Telugu and Urdu. In 1967, vide 21st amendment to the Indian Constitution, Sindhi was also included in the Scheduled Languages. Another two amendments in the Indian Constitution in 1992 and 2003 added seven more languages as part of the Scheduled Languages. The latest additions are Konkani, Manipuri, Nepali, Bodo, Dogri, Santhali and Maithali making a total of 22 Scheduled Languages.

It should be noted that Dogri language was included as part of the Scheduled Languages in 2003. One complete section in this book has been devoted to this language as well as Dogra culture.

Coming on to the Non-Scheduled languages, currently there are 99 such languages whereas in the census of 2001, there were 100 languages. Actually, the number of speakers of two languages Simte and Persian got reduced below 10,000 and hence these were removed from the list of Non-Scheduled languages and one language Mao where the speakers became more than 10,000 got included in the census of 2011.

Regarding popularity of languages, Hindi is the most widely spoken language, besides it being the official language along with English. According to PrintWeek, India is the third largest publisher of books in the English language globally. Other languages are the regional languages and are spoken within the states.

Geographical Diversity

India is a very vast country with landscapes ranging from snow-capped mountains to deserts, plain areas, grassy lands, hills and plateaus. The mountains of Himalayas cover its northern part and are the major source of big rivers. The plains have rivers Ganga, Jamuna, Godavari and many more which irrigate the farmlands and are also a source of transportation in many regions.

Most of the population in the country are believers of Hindu religion and they worship nature including the rivers. Every day in the morning, while taking the bath, they chant a *Sanskrit Shlok*:

"Gange cha Yamune chaiv Godavari, Saraswati, Narmade,
Sindhu, Kaveri, Jalesmin Sannadhim Kuru"

In this *Shlok*, they say, "In this water, I invoke the presence of divine waters from Rivers Ganga, Yamuna, Godavari, Saraswati, Narmada, Sindhu and Kaveri, pray these and get their blessings" Hindus consider these rivers as Goddesses and pray to these on many of their ritual functions.

On the Western side of the country, in the State of Rajasthan, there is a vast land of deserts whereas Eastern India is full of forests and hills. Three sides of Southern India touch Indian Ocean, Bay of Bengal and Arabian Sea, and have got tropical jungles, coastal areas and beaches which add to its charms.

The country has thousands of small villages and towns, each with its own culture. Metro cities like Delhi, Kolkata, Madras, Mumbai have populations of over 10 million each and are economic hubs. Within these metros, the people still maintain and preserve their own cultural identity.

Religious Diversity

The Constitution of India declares the country as a secular one and hence everyone has the right to follow any religion. According to the 2011 census, the majority population is that of Hindus (around 80%), followed by Muslims (14.2%), Christians (1.7%), Sikhs (1.7%), Buddhists (0.7%) and Jains (0.4%).

Within each religion there are further subdivisions. Hindus are further divided into Brahmins, Rajputs, Kshtryas, Jats, Yadavs, scheduled castes etc. Similarly, within Muslims, there are Sunnies, Shiites, Sufies, Wahhabis, Deobandi etc.

Hindus can be traced in all the parts of India whereas Shia Muslims are concentrated in Gujarat, Sunnis in Jammu and Kashmir, U.P., West Bengal, Kerala and other major cities. Most Sikhs reside in Punjab and northern India, Buddhists in Maharashtra, and Christians in Kerala,

Tamil Nadu and Meghalaya. However, the presence of each religion, may be in smaller numbers, could be found in almost all the towns of India.

Each religion has its peculiarities with respect to architecture, culture, artistry and society. Whereas Islam is a monotheistic faith and adheres to Sharia law, Hinduism is a polytheistic faith whose followers follow religious laws called Dharma. Hindus believe in rebirth, *murti puja,* and rewards based on one's *karmas* whereas Muslims discard murti *puja.*

So religious diversity is seen in all parts of the country.

Quotes on Indian Religious Diversity

India is a country in which every great religion finds a home.

– Annie Besant, British Socialist
and One of the Founders of Banaras Hindu University

To other countries, I may go as a tourist, but to India, I come as a pilgrim.

– Nobel Laureate Martin Luther King Jr.

Ethnic and Tribal diversity

India is a diverse multiethnic country and home to thousands of big and small ethnic and tribal groups. The main two ethnic groups are Indo-Aryan who stay mostly in the northern parts of India and Dravidian who live in Southern India. Within each ethnic group, the cultural diversity is very vast. For example, Indo-Aryans are Assamese, Gujaratis, Kashmiris, Marathas, and Punjabis etc. and each of which has a totally different culture. Similar is the case with Dravidian ethnic groups where we find Tamilians, Telugus, Kannada, Malayalees with different languages and cultures.

Similarly, there are as many as 550 tribes in India, each having its own distinct culture. According to the 2011 census, the population of scheduled tribes was around 8.6% of the country's population and they were over 104 million in number. The eastern states of India like Mizoram, Nagaland, Meghalaya and Arunachal Pradesh have sizable numbers of tribal population whereas they are also found in the States of Bihar, Uttar Pradesh, Tamil Nadu, Kerala and Uttara Khand. Most of them live in urban areas whereas only one million stay in rural areas.

Bhil is the largest of all the tribal groups in India and constitute approximately 38% of the total scheduled tribal population. Cuisine, handicraft, dresses and methods of recreation in each ethnic group are different.

Diversity due to settlement by Foreigners

Over the centuries, citizens and tribes from many countries settled in India. Though most of them merged with the local culture, still some of them maintain their own culture and speak their own languages. A few of these are mentioned below:

a. Portuguese in Goa
b. Negros in Andaman Nicobar
c. Afghans
d. Persians
e. Many tribes in the Union Territory of Andaman and Nicobar who migrated from many mainlands.
f. Tibetans

Miscellaneous Cultural Diversity

Besides the above, there is diversity in every aspect of life, whether it is music, dance, clothing, festival etc. The dance form *Bhangra* is performed by Punjabis whereas classical dances *Kathak* and *Bharatanatyam* are performed in Uttar Pradesh and Tamil Nadu respectively. Folk dances *Bihu* and *Garba* are popular with Assamese and Gujaratis respectively.

As in dances, one finds diversity in festivals, dresses, culinary habits etc. in the country. Glimpses of a few of these diversities are depicted pictorially as under:

a. Diversity in festivals: The biggest religion in India is Hindu. Their main festival is Kumb Mela in which hundreds of million Hindus participate. In the Kumbh Mela held at Prayagraj during January-February 2025, around 660 million Hindus participated and took holy bath in Sangam. A picture of two of the co-authors of this book who also participated in Kumbh Mela is at Fig. 6.1. Diversity in some of the other festivals is depicted on Fig. 6.2.

b. Diversity in dresses (Fig. 6.3)

c. Diversity in traditional dances (Fig. 6.4)

Fig 6.1: Two co-authors of the book, viz. Aarti Sharma and Shiv Kumar participating in the biggest festival of Hindus *Kumbh Mela* at Prayagraj during Jan-Feb 2025

Diverse Festivals in India

Lohri in Punjab and Jammu

Eid-Ul-Fitr by Muslims

Durga Puja in West Bengal

Holi in Bihar, Uttar Pradesh etc.

Pongal in Kerala

Fig. 6.2: Diversity of festivals in India

Fig. 6.3: Dress diversity in India
(Source: Wikipedia)

Fig. 6.4: Various dance forms in India
(Source: Websites of Govt. departments and Britannica)

ENDANGERED CULTURES IN INDIA

Those parents who neither teach the native language to their children at home nor use it actively in everyday affairs, are the ones responsible for making their culture die down.

A common saying

Can you believe that close to 250 languages in India died in the past 60 years and another 600 are dying in the next decade or so? Is it believable that the tribe Jarawa had only 380 people left in 2011 whereas Onge and Great Andamanese tribes were left with still a smaller number of people i.e, 101 and 52 respectively. Doesn't it appear to be shocking?

Bo, a language in Andaman, disappeared in 2010 and *Majhi* language of Sikkim disappeared in 2015. Similarly, there used to be many other languages like Adhuni, Ghallu, Katagi, Helgo and Dichi, in various states of India, which have become extinct now. When a language disappears, it takes away with it the complete treasure of cultural wealth, skills and civilization associated with it. Let us look at various linguistic surveys carried out within India in the last two centuries.

Linguistic Survey of India

The concept of a comprehensive survey of languages of India originated way back in 1886 by George Abraham Grierson, an ICS and a linguist who attended the International Oriental Congress in Vienna. He made a proposal for the survey, which was initially rejected by the then government, but later in 1891, it got formal approval. On the ground, it commenced in 1894 and continued for 30 years and results were published in 1928.

A project on *The Second Linguistic Survey of India* was initiated by the Languages Division of the Office of the Registrar General and Census Commissioner of India in 1984. Till 2010, only 40% of the survey was completed.

In the meantime, in 2010, an NGO named Bhasha Research and Publications Centre, Vadodara with Mr. Ganesh N. Devy as its Chairman started a survey named People's Linguistic Survey of India (PLSI). Another organization, Adivasi Academy at Tejgarh, Gujarat documented 780 living languages of India and pointed out that the country has already lost 220 languages since 1961. They also brought out that another 400 of these are in danger of becoming extinct. Let us now evaluate the endangerment of languages in contemporary India based on the official documents made available by the government.

The matter regarding the endangered languages in India had figured in Lok Sabha on 24th of June 2019. The Minister replied that UNESCO had published *Atlas of the World's Languages in Danger* in 2010 in which 197 Indian languages had been shown in the endangered category. A language spoken by less than 10,000 people is considered a potentially endangered language.

Census of India 2011

Latest Census of Population in India was conducted in 2011 in which details of all the languages spoken in the country were documented. Its report was published in 2018 as *Paper 1 of 2018 LANGUAGE India, States and Union Territories (Table C-16)*. Next Census has not yet started till publication of this book.

As per the Census report, the population of India was 1.21 billion in 2011, with 19,569 mother tongues spoken by them. Each mother tongue has a distinct culture associated with it. After linguistic scrutiny and rationalization these were grouped as under:

a. Rationalized languages = 1,369
b. Unclassified other mother tongues = 1,474

Out of the 1,369 rationalized mother tongues, only 270 mother tongues were spoken by over 10,000 persons. After the census of India conducted in 1971, the Indian government declared that any language spoken by less than 10,000 people need not be included in the official list of languages. So, it is seen that most of the minor languages are not considered for planning purposes. However, these 1,369 were further clubbed following usual linguistic method as under:

a. 123 mother tongues were grouped in 22 major languages and included in the Eighth Schedule of the Indian Constitution. These are called Scheduled Languages.
b. Balance 147 mother tongues were also grouped in 99 languages and called as the non-scheduled languages in the Constitution of India.

Origin of Indian Languages

Based on the origin of the languages, the Scheduled and Non-Scheduled languages, as contained in the Constitution of India which total up to 121 belong to 5 language families. The number of languages in each of the families are given below:

a. Indo European Family of Languages comprising of
   - Indo-Aryan   - 21 (North, East, West and Central Indian languages)
   - Iranian   - 1 (Afghani/Kabuli/Pushto)
   - Germanic   - 1 (English)

b. Dravidian   - 17 (South Indian Languages)
c. Austro Asiatic   - 14
d. Tibeto-Burmese   - 66
e. Semito-Hamintic   - 1 (Arbi/Arabic)

Endangered Languages

As already mentioned, the *Bo* language of Andaman vanished in 2010, while Sikkim's Majhi language became extinct in 2015. In 2018, UNESCO came out with another report, as per which the following 11 languages in India have already become dead on ground. These are:

- Wadari, Kolhati, Golla and Gisari (Spoken in Maharashtra, Karnataka and Telengana)
- Pauri, Korku, Haldi and Mivchi spoken in Central India
- Moran, Tangsa, Aiton spoken in Assam

In the Census-2011 report, all the languages in the category of "Other mother tongues" and the 1,099 (=1,369-270) rationalized languages are spoken by less than 10,000 persons. However, as per the latest report by UNESCO published in 2018, there are 42 languages which are spoken by less than 10,000 persons as per the report. The list of the languages State/UT wise are given at Table 7.1.

Table: 7.1: Languages with speaker strength less than 10,000

S.No.	State/UT	Language or place of extinction of Language being spoken by less than 10,000 persons
1.	Andaman & Nicobar Islands	Great Andamanese, Jarawa, Lamongse, Luro, Muot, Onge, Pu, Sanenyo, Sentilese, Shompen and Takahanyilang (11 languages)
2.	Manipur	Aimol, Aka, Koiren, Lamgang, Langrong, Purum and Tarao (7 languages)
3.	Himachal Pradesh	Baghati, Handuri, Pangvali and Sirmaudi (4 languages)
4.	Odisha	Manda, Parji and Pengo (3 Languages)
5.	Karnataka	Koraga and Kadu-Kuruba (2 languages)
6.	Andhra Pradesh	Gadaba and Naiki (2 languages)
7.	Tamil Nadu	Kota and Toda (2 languages)
8.	Arunachal Pradesh	Mra and Na (2 languages)
9.	Assam	Tai Nora and Tai Rong (2 languages)
10.	Uttarakhand	Bangani
11.	Jharkhand	Birhor
12.	Maharashtra	Nihali
13.	Meghalaya	Ruga
14.	West Bengal	Toto

Now let us look at the other 20 endangered languages which are spoken by more than 10,000 people but less than 30,000 and these are tabulated at Tables 7.2 and 7.3.

Table 7.2: Indian languages with speaker strength between 10,000 and 20,000 persons

S.No.	Name of Language	Number of Speakers
1.	Seema	10,802
2.	Lahauli	11,574
3.	Monpa	13,703
4.	Balti	13,744
5.	Ladhaki	14,952
6.	Kom	15,108
7.	Rai	15644
8.	Sherpa	16,016
9	Gangte	16,542
10.	Chakhesana	19,846

Table 7.3: Indian languages with speaker strength between 20,000 and 30,000 persons

S.No.	Name of Language	Number of Speakers
1.	Jatapu	20,028
2.	Tamang	20,154
3.	Pochur	21,654
4.	Afgani/Pushto/Kabuli	21,677
5.	Moring	25,810
6.	Zou	26,545
7.	Anal	27,217
8.	Bhumij	27,506
9.	Pawi	28,099
10.	Ncobarese	29,099

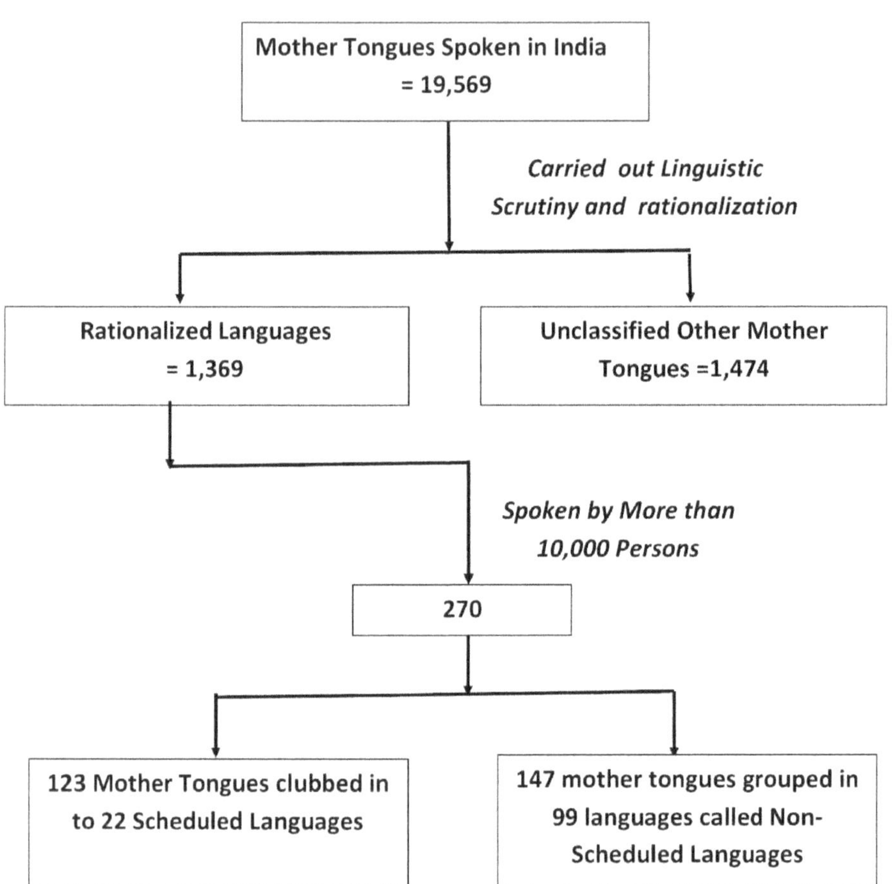

Fig 7.1: Analysis of Indian languages based on Census-2011
(Source: Census Report -2011 by Govt. of India)

Number of Speakers of
Scheduled Languages in India

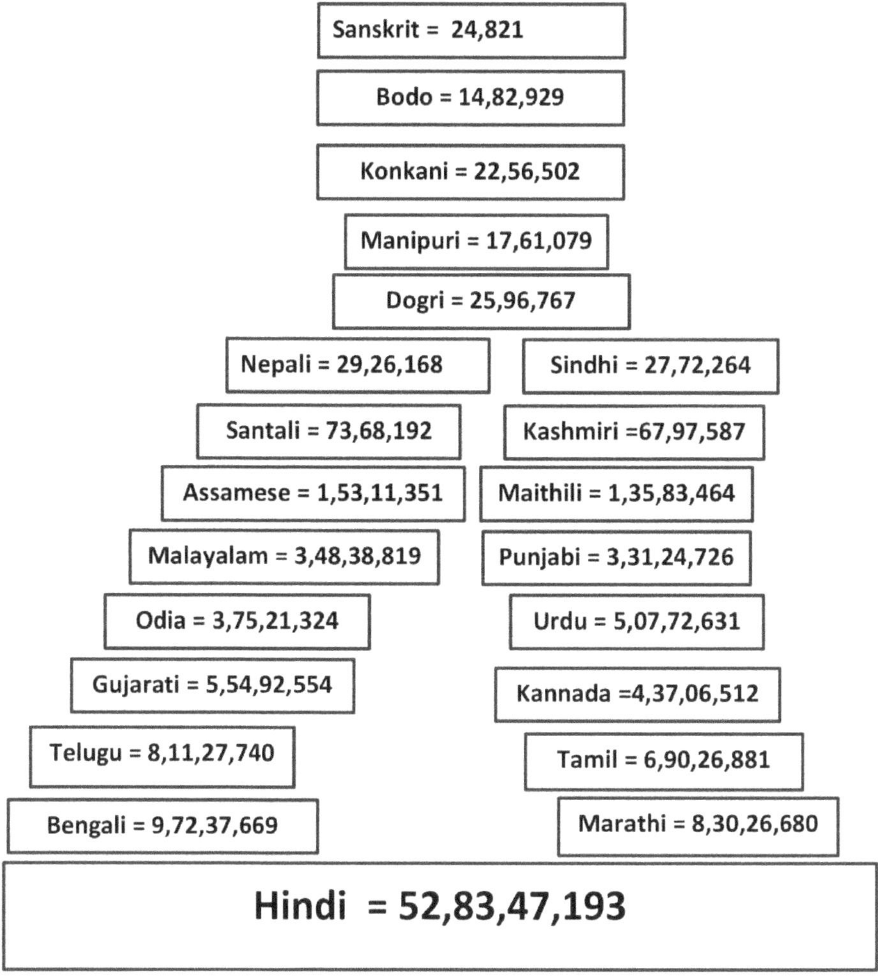

Fig. 7.2: Number of speakers of each of the Scheduled languages in India
(Source: Census Report -2011 by Govt. of India)

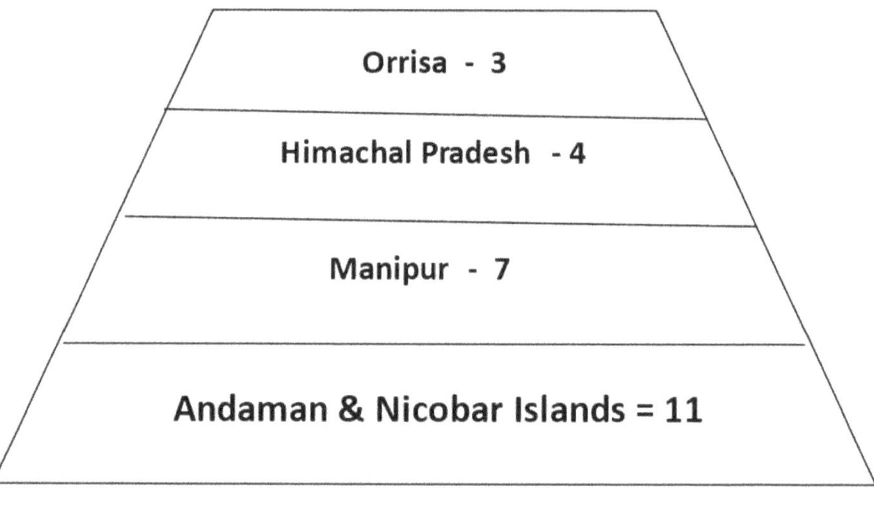

Fig 7.3: State wise number of endangered languages in India
(*Source:* www.indiatoday.in, *21 Feb 2018))*

Chapter 8

INDIAN GOVT'S INITIATIVES TO SAVE ENDANGERED CULTURES

Indigenous languages are central to our cultures, our life ways, and who we are as people. They connect us to our ancestors, to our homelands and to our place in the world.

– Deb Haaland,
Secretary of the Interior, USA

The Constitution of India lays ample safeguards to conserve languages, scripts and cultures so that minorities do not get neglected. This provision has been kept in Article 29 of the Indian Constitution. Accordingly, the Govt. of India, the State Govts./Union Territories, educational institutions as well as civil society have taken various initiatives to preserve the endangered and lesser known languages.

Initiatives by Government of India

The Ministry of Education as well as the Ministry of Tribal Affairs, Government of India have established certain centers/institutes and started many schemes to address these problems and preserve the endangered cultures. Some of these are:

a. **Central Institute of Indian Languages (CIIL)**: It has been established under the Ministry of Education, Govt. of India with the responsibility to protect and document all languages including the tribal and endangered languages. In 2013, CIIL initiated a program named *Scheme for Protection and Preservation of Endangered Languages* (SPPEL) to save and preserve through digital documentation and archive the languages that have been endangered or likely to be endangered.

b. **Tribal Research Institutes (TRIs)**: These have been established by the Ministry of Tribal Affairs, Govt. of India with the mandate to identify, enlist and preserve the endangered languages. This Ministry also extends support to State Governments/UTs for developing bilingual Primers for enhancement of learning achievement level among the Scheduled Tribe students. Till 2019, various state governments had developed Primers for 82 languages.

c. **Scheme for Safeguarding Intangible Heritage and Diverse Traditions of India**: Under this scheme, substantial financial and infrastructural support is provided for the preservation and promotion of India's traditions, performing arts, and social practices. Various heritage sites in the country are identified and their preservation is ensured under this scheme.

d. **Initiatives by University Grants Commission (UGC)**: This Commission is a statutory body in India which coordinates all aspects of higher education in the country. It lays down standards of higher education and provides recognition to the Universities. It also gives financial aid to higher educational institutions.

It has initiated two schemes for the protection of endangered languages and detailed guidelines have been issued to the universities. Provisions have been made for the establishment of centers, exclusively for endangered languages, and appropriate funding provisions have been catered for. These are:

i. Establishment of Centers for Endangered Languages in Central Universities

ii. Funding support to the State Universities for study and research in indigenous and endangered languages in India.

e. **Promotion through National Education Policy-2020**: The Ministry of Education has already taken steps to strengthen the local languages through the 3-Language schooling formula. It will help children to understand the basics of the subjects in an easier way through their native language as well as nurture the growth of traditional language.

f. **Fund Support by Govt. of India**: During the initial period of 4 years i.e. 2015-16 to 2019-2020, amount allotted to various universities and schemes was as under:

i.   Central Universities   - Rs. 26.10 crore

ii. State Universities   - Rs. 10.35 crore

iii. SPPEL (CIIL)   - Rs. 9.44 crore

For endangered languages, a lot of work has been done by various institutes, the state governments and social organizations, some of which have been covered here.

Activities Under SPPEL

The Scheme for Protection and Preservation of Endangered Languages (SPPEL) was launched by CIIL in 2013 with the aim to save and preserve through digital documentation and archive the languages that have been endangered or likely to be endangered.

This scheme is governed by a core committee headed by Director CIIL, Mysuru, Karnataka and 12 core members who are Vice Chancellors/professors from various universities connected with the departments of linguistics and culture.

In the first phase, it has listed 117 languages, spoken by less than 10,000 speakers, for their documentation. Each of these languages is placed under one of the six zones of the country viz. North, South, Northeast, East Central, Western Central and Andaman-Nicobar. It is seen that out of 117 endangered languages, 43 endangered languages are in the Northeast Zone, followed by 25 in the Northern Zone. Balance 49 endangered languages are being studied at other four zones. The number of languages to be studied, zone-wise, is given at Table 8.1.

Table: 8.1: Number of endangered languages being studied Zone-wise

S.No.	Zone	Number of Endangered Languages
1.	North	25
2.	West-Central	5
3.	South	20
4.	East Central	15
5.	North-East	43
6.	Andaman Nicobar	9
Total		117

SPPEL is performing this task of documentation in an excellent way. Firstly, it prepares a tri-lingual dictionary of the language, then its grammar and finally the ethno-linguistic profile of that community.

The process of collecting this data is by way of sending a questionnaire to the public with the aim of collecting information about features of the language and the people. They collect all types of sentences highlighting the different grammatical aspects of each language.

They also prepare visual and audio features of culturally significant items such as housing, artifacts, cultivation, healing and ritual practices, festivals, occupation, customs, folk songs and folklores etc.

To have a feel of the quality of work being done by SPPEL, an example of one such endangered language named *Khash*, spoken in the Doda region of J&K State is attached at Appendix A. It can be noticed from there the details to which the teams are going to capture each aspect of the language so that it can be preserved.

Activities of Centre for Endangered Languages (CEL) at IGNTU

CEL was established under Indira Gandhi National Tribal University in 2015 to undertake documentation and revitalization projects in the states with a tribal population of 50 lacs or above such as Madhya Pradesh, Maharashtra, Gujarat, Andhra Pradesh, Telangana and Rajasthan. A project named "Endangered Languages Project" has been granted by the UGC to prevent the endangerment and extinction of tribal languages. It is to document and record various aspects of the language, carry out linguistic data analysis etc. to enhance the possibilities of tribal languages to be part of the mainstream by making these unwritten languages available in published and digitized form

The Centre is focused on studying the languages spoken by some indigenous communities in the central Indian State of Madhya Pradesh and in other states such as Maharashtra, Gujarat, Andhra Pradesh, Telangana and Rajasthan.

Activities of Centre for Endangered Languages (CEL) at Tejpur University

CEL was established with the aim of conducting substantial research on the lesser known and endangered languages of Northeast India and to revitalize them with direct and indirect institutional intervention. It has already started working and giving output. Some of the completed works are as under:

a. Developed the first version of the Trilingual Dictionary Android Apps for four languages namely Biate, Khelma, Purum and Yimkhiung.

b. Produced Learners' books for 7 languages

c. Prepared ethnolinguistic study for 7 languages

d. Prepared draft dictionaries for 7 languages

e. Conducted in numerous conferences and workshops on lesser-known languages of North-east states

Actions by Various State Governments

1. **State Govt of Odisha:** Odisha has one of the most diverse tribal populations in India, with 62 tribes, including 13 particularly vulnerable tribal groups. There are 21 tribal languages and 74 dialects which immensely contribute to the linguistic diversity of the State. There are only six tribal languages which have a written script.

   The state government adopted the Multi-Lingual Education (MLE) program in 2006 to address the issues of language barriers faced by tribal children. The government has appointed 3,385 tribal language teachers for the MLE program. Additionally, the state government published dictionaries for 20 tribal languages. These not only enable scholars and enthusiasts to learn languages but also produce literature, ultimately, conserving the existing ones.

   Under the scheme "First Language First" the Government of Odisha has conducted the MLE (multilingual education) program on 1485 tribal schools in 21 recorded tribal languages of the state. For teaching materials, *Ol-Chiki* script (for Santhali) is being introduced as well as 3400 *Shiksha Sahayaks* and 242 Language Instructors have been appointed.

2. **State Govt of Chhattisgarh:** The Language and Learning Foundation initiated India's first "Language Mapping of Schools" survey in Chhattisgarh. The study was conducted in partnership with the Government of Chhattisgarh and UNICEF Bharat as part of the NIPUN Bharat program, and around 30,000 schools were surveyed. According to the poll, around 75% of kids are expected to encounter medium to significant educational disadvantages as a result of the gap between their native tongue and the school language utilized as their means of teaching. It also reveals that around 95% of pupils entering elementary schools communicate in their mother tongue language other than Hindi depicting the importance of the preservation and spread of native language in terms of communication.

3. **State Govt. of Sikkim:** Mr. Gideon Taso Lepcha, is working on reviving and digitizing the Lepcha language. He started *"Rongring,"* a Lepcha Language Online Global course in 2020 and formed a team of experts to develop an LMS (Learning Management System) to learn the language online. There were 90% of Lepcha language speakers in villages who didn't know how to read and write. Hence, to make the language accessible and simplified, Gideon designed and developed a framework called "Wangboo" that can enable any learner to learn the language within 10 hours.

   It is to remind that a program named *Rongring* became very popular as an e-learning platform and it was successfully used to teach the Lepcha language to students across 13 countries (Japan, Italy, Canada, North America, Maldives, Czech Republic, Switzerland, Holland, Bhutan, New Zealand, Nepal, India & U.K) within a year of its formation.

4. **State Govt. of Andhra Pradesh:** Similar kinds of approaches have also been taken in the tribal-dominated area of Andhra Pradesh where 1,350 schools are implementing schemes similar to MLE for training in languages like Koya, Savara, Adivasi Oria, Jatapu, Kuvi, and Konda Dora.

5. **State Govt. of Jharkhand:** 1,000 schools in 8 districts are nominated for the mother-tongue-based multilingual education where books have been translated already into 5 tribal languages viz. Santhali, Mundari, Ho, Kurukh, and Kharia

6. **State Govts. of Northeastern States:** Banwang Losu, a schoolteacher from Arunachal Pradesh's Longding district, has created a Unicode script for the Wancho language, which is spoken by the Wancho tribe in Arunachal Pradesh, Assam, Nagaland, and Myanmar. It consists of 29 consonants and 15 vowels. The languages have also been introduced in primary and upper primary schools by the Government of Arunachal Pradesh. Simultaneously, the Centre for Endangered Languages, Rajiv Gandhi University of Arunachal Pradesh developed a basic grammatical sketch for many languages.

7. **State Govt. of Tamil Nadu:** *Badagas* and *Saurashtrians* represent unique ethnic groups in the State of Tamil Nadu. *Badaga* is a 2,300-year-old Dravidian language spoken by the *Badaga* people in the Nilgiris and bears striking similarities to Kannada, but it does not have any script. UNESCO has classified *Badaga* under the category of "Definitely Endangered Languages.

Similarly, *Saurashtra* is a language of the Indo-Aryan family spoken by the Gujarati Hindu Brahmin community that migrated to Tamil Nadu from southern Gujarat after the fall of Somnath Temple in the 11th Century. Many them were the weavers.

During Feb 2024, the Govt of Tamil Nadu, allocated Rs. 20 million towards preservation of these languages in addition to other endangered languages used by tribes like *Todar, Kothar, Solagar, Kani, Narikuravars* etc.

8. **State Govt. of Himachal Pradesh:** Most of the Pahari languages in the State of Himachal Pradesh are neither the official languages nor any priority given to these. So, some of these have come in the endangered list of languages by UNESCO. *Kullui*, a language of the Kullu district of Himachal Pradesh is one of such languages.

This language is mainly used for oral communication in many villages and has no standardized script as of today. However, before the 20th century, this language was written in Takri script (a common script for *Pahari* languages including Dogri language).

A Project to document all Himachali languages was started in 2014 in the Institute of Linguistics, Russian Academy of Sciences. Its main aim is to finalize grammatical description of *Kullui* language, make its dictionary, teaching material, language documentation with audio visual recordings. Since 2014, many expeditions of the Institute have taken place in various villages where this language is spoken, and documentation has been done. It is believed that the work will be completed shortly.

9. **State Govt of J&K:** In the State of Jammu and Kashmir, there are many languages which are in the endangered list and have no status in the government. Some of these languages are Bakarwali, Gojri, Bhadarwahi, Shiraji etc.

   The govt. has opened an Academy named J&K Academy of Art, Culture and Languages. This academy is fully staffed and conducts many programs to keep the languages of the state alive. Details of this academy will be covered under the Chapter of Dogri Languages.

10. **State Govt. of Karnataka:** There are many languages like Kulu, Koracha, Aruvumu, Pardi, Gondi, Gyari, Korage etc. which are spoken in the State of Karnataka but have no proper documentation, grammar etc. These are spoken by large communities and need to be preserved.

    The Govt. of Karnataka has established a Centre for Endangered Languages in the Central University of Karnataka which is working on these languages. During February 2023, they conducted an international training program on language documentation of the endangered Languages.

    Till date they have published sketch grammar for six minor languages and plan to produce documentaries, text materials and other materials for the same languages.

11. **Govt. of Gujarat:** There are 25 tribes (earlier 30 communities) in Gujarat including 5 primitive tribes. To preserve and promote these tribes, Govt. of Gujarat has formed a society named *The Gujarat Tribal Research and Training Society.* It was established in 1962 and carries out field studies on the tribal structure, demographic features, socio-economic conditions etc. of these tribes. The research findings are utilized in formulating plans for development and enriching the contents and quality of the training programmes.

Appendix A

Khash, An Endangered Language of J&K State, India:
Extracts of the Work done by SPPEL on *Khash*

Where is the language spoken?

Khash language is spoken in village Sarsi-Daryan, located in the District Doda of Jammu and Kashmir State, India. The village is 40 kms away from the main city of Doda.

Population of the Community

Khash language is one of the members of the Indo-Aryan language family and spoken by Hindus of the region. The speakers of *Khash* language are less than 500, and hence it is one of the endangered languages in India.

Other Neighboring Societies

The population of Sarsi village is around 1100, out of which 700-750 people are Muslims and the rest 350-400 are Hindus. The village is known not only for its cultural heritage and ethnic values, but also for its secularism and religious tolerance. The languages spoken in Sarsi village panchayats are mostly Kashmiri, which is spoken by Muslims.

Although some Muslims can also speak *Khash*, but it is not their native language. Other than Kashmiri and *Khash*, the people of Sarsi village know Urdu and Hindi. Urdu is the lingua-franca of the area.

Religion and Occupation

The people of the Khash community belong to Hinduism. They worship gods and goddesses of the Hindu religion. The main concept regarding the substantive belief revolves around the faith in Kul Devta (a name assigned to Lord Shiva) and Kul Devi (Khol). While worshipping Lord

Shiva is almost a common practice in Hinduism, Khash people differ from other Hindus in worshipping Khol as their Kul Devi. The main and grand ritual called Yag popularly known as Khadal (kʰaɖaːl) in Khash community of Sarsi-Daryan is performed during night to please Lord Shiva. In this ritual the devotees mainly worship the *Shivlinga* to praise and thank the God.

Occupation of People

Agriculture is the main occupation of the Khash people. The major crops grown by the Khash people are maize and rice. There are other occupations like wood cutting, cattle grazing, etc., mostly done by the male folk of the community

Script of the Language

Khash language has no script and is not taught in any of the local schools. There is no available literature in Khash language, but the language is rich in oral tradition, folk songs and folklore. No linguistic research or documentation of this language has been done till date. It remains unexplored as far as the linguistic description of the language is concerned.

Further Work being Undertaken under SPPEL

At present the documentation and description of the language is going on. It includes providing a brief grammatical sketch of the language and compilation of the pictorial dictionary of the language. The work to document the ethnolinguistic profile of the community is undergoing. The domains like stories, narratives, folklore, transportation, games and entertainment, religion and rituals, social customs and communicative behavior are yet to be completed. The documentation of various aspects of Khash language and community is being done in audio and video forms.

Village Houses and Occupation

Shoes

Vegetable Cutter

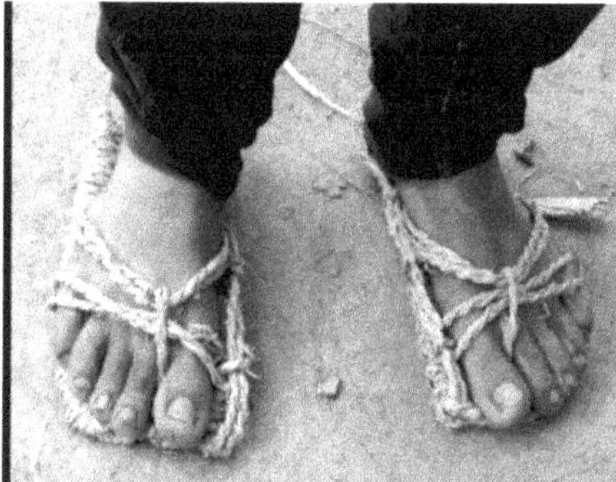

Ladies Ornaments

Fig. 8.1: Some typical photos of Sarsi Village of J&K, India where inhabitants speak *Khash* language which is in the Endangered list of Languages

Chapter 9

EFFORTS OF CIVIL SOCIETY TO SAVE LOCAL LANGUAGES

*"The most important thing to me is to teach the children,
so that our culture never dies."*

- Dottie LeBeau, USA

In India, the citizens are very much attached to their cultures. They are very possessive about their culture and want their children to follow that. Most of the elderly people speak in their home language with their children, which carries forward the native language to next generations.

It is commonly seen that during vacations, elders take their children to religious places or heritage places for their entertainment and making them aware of the native culture. In the *Maha Kumbh* festival at Prayagraj, India during Jan-Feb 2025, the number of people, mainly from Hindu families, who took dip in Holy *Sangam* at Triveni, Prayagraj was over 650 million which is equivalent to half of their population in the world.

Elders and children also take part in the local festivals in which they wear traditional dresses, sing their native songs and perform native dances. Children, when they grow old, also repeat this and thus cultural traits are transmitted from one generation to the next.

Most of the schools and colleges celebrate their annual days in which songs, dances and skits are performed in the local language. One day in a year, generally, grandfathers are invited, firstly to entertain them, and secondly to make the children understand the value of the enormous cultural wealth.

This ultimately helps in keeping the culture alive and transmitting it to the next generations.

Contributions of Indian communities in revitalizing endangered languages and preserving their local culture can be summarized as under:

- Speaking to their children in their native language
- Participating in local festivals and organizing cultural events in the neighborhood. In India, kite festivals, *gidda, bhangra, dusherrah, pon*gal etc. are celebrated by the local communities within their respective communities/regions.
- All the local rituals within communities are celebrated with local customs and traditions. For example, in marriages in the communities, it is very common for the ladies and gents to sing songs in their native language and the dances are performed as per their tradition. Even rituals like *puja* are done as per the cultural traditions. The chanting of religious *bhajans*, performance of puja by traditional religious preachers are all in the local vernacular. As it is an ongoing process, this helps in transmission of culture from generation to generation thus saving cultural flavor in society.
- Films are made in local languages and even the TV programmes and uploading material on social media like YouTube etc. are done in the local language.
- Writing books in the local language and creating a wealth of literature.
- Celebrating family functions elaborately in which all the activities are performed as per the local customs and traditions.
- Economically sound elderly people create economic opportunities for the communities by employing their community people in their business houses. Generally, there is a higher degree of trust

in the people of their own community than in other communities. They also take help from their native employees in their traditional functions.

NGOs for preservation of Cultures

Understanding the need to preserve endangered languages, civil society also comes forward, forms various Non-Govt. Organizations (NGOs), Non-Profit Organizations (NPOs), cultural and social societies and conduct activities which support the local cultures. A few of the prominent organizations in various States of India are listed here along with a brief about a few of these:

a. **In The States of UP and Uttarakhand:** A very prestigious organization which works in both states is ***Society for Endangered and Lesser-Known Languages (SEL).*** It is an NGO that was established in July 2011 and registered in March 2015 by Dr. Kavita Rastogi, a Professor of Linguistics in the University of Lucknow, India. With the help of like-minded people, this NGO studies various endangered languages in both these states and other neighboring states too, prepares documents, describes their grammar, prepares dictionaries and pedagogical material for the native communities.

   It has already completed work on the communities/languages like *Raji* (a tribal community inhabited in 11 small hamlets in the State of Uttarakhand, India), *Todpa, Punan, Pattani and Spiti.*

   Seeing the dedication of Dr. Rastogi, many volunteers have joined this NGO. Her famous quote is

   "If you want to do something significant, build your own path."

   Similarly, listed below are the cultural organizations, popular in various states of India.

b. **In West Bengal:** A few of the Kolkata-based cultural organizations which promote local languages, customs and traditions by conducting cultural programmes, skits, plays etc. in the native languages and keep these alive are:

i. Shanti Cultural Club

ii. Bhartiya Sanskriti Sangam

iii. Eastern Zone Cultural Centre

iv. Shanti Chakra Club

c. **In Gujarat**

i. Adivasi Academy, Tejgadh, Gujarat: This academy was opened as a project under Bhasha Research and Publication Centre. This academy organizes cultural performances, festivals, theatre, songs and rituals in the local language. It also documents folklore of the Adivasi people. To train a greater number of people in tribal culture, it offers academic courses including a Post-Graduate Diploma in Tribal Culture and Development.

ii. *Ashramshalas*: These are the schools where schooling, boarding and lodging facilities are provided to the children of Schedule Tribes, free of cost, so that they can get better employment and compete in society. Close to 600 such *Ashramshalas* are run providing these facilities to more than 80,000 students annually.

iii. Cultural Club in Educational Institutions: Almost every college in Gujarat has a cultural club where they showcase the cultural acumen of all the cultures in Gujarat thus promoting each and every culture.

d. **In Tamil Nadu:** A few of the organizations where cultural programmes are held are as under:

i. Sadhana Cultural Academy

ii. Green Glen Cultural Association

iii. WCA - Whitefield Kali Pujo

iv. New Acropolis Cultural organization

e. **In Manipur:** Similarly, a few of the societies which promote cultural activities are given below:

    i.   Community Builders Society
    ii. Indo-Myanmar Tribal Development Association (IMTDA)
    iii. Action for Welfare and Awakening in rural Environment, Imphal
    iv. Rural Development Society

NGOs in Tribal Areas

In India, tribes are scattered generally in the hilly and forest areas. The tribal people had been deprived of good education, urban facilities and most of them had remained backwards. Those who stay near the urban areas tend to adopt culture prevalent in the cities, assuming that to be an advanced culture which would provide them with more facilities and recognition. In the bargain, the number of people speaking the original language dwindles. It is seen that most tribal languages have already become extinct, and many are at the verge of extinction.

NGOs have realized that if good education, health facilities, and business opportunities are made available to them in their own villages and towns, then this would help save these cultures. Six prominent NGOs which are working for welfare are described below.

a. **Tribal Cooperative Marketing Development Federation (TRIFED):** This NGO focuses on endogenous tribes. Their marketing initiatives enable tribes to sell their products in the market thus helping them achieve economic stability. The products from arts and crafts to creams and even alcoholic beverages which are generally prepared by tribes are sold in the market. The federation also provides its marketing expertise to connect tribes to the rest of the country, thus increasing their visibility and getting enhanced sales of their products. It also provides them with facilities to develop skills on supply chain management for tapping the bigger market.

b. **Adivasi Foundation**: This Foundation is involved in building socioeconomic structure of the tribal areas through the initiatives in education, healthcare and economic opportunities. It provides scholarships to meritorious people, education facilities and builds infrastructure.

The Foundation also conducts awareness campaigns for healthy living and provides healthcare facilities. It gives opportunities for their economic empowerment. The impact of the Foundation has been visible in these areas and thus saving their culture and dissuading them from adopting other cultures.

c. **The Tribal Initiative:** This initiative focuses specifically on tribal healthcare. Some of the key programmes initiated by this Initiative are:
   - Organizing health camps
   - Providing medical assistance in remote regions
   - Spreading awareness on healthcare and hygiene
   - Relief and disease management

Its impact has been seen on the ground with the improved health of the tribal people coupled with a higher sense of awareness through community engagement.

d. **The Centre for Tribal and Rural Development (CTRD):** This Centre was created to provide a more holistic approach to the tribal communities with a mission to induce sustainable development among tribal groups. It undertakes the following key programmes:
   - Sanitation programmes
   - Setting up hospitals and medical centers
   - Development of infrastructural facilities for education and general development
   - Economic development programmes

The impact of the programmes of CTRD is very visible and can be seen from the improved lifestyle of tribal communities and better health awareness. Their economic condition has improved, and society has become more resilient to modern changes.

e. **Gram Vikas**: This initiative is also for the development of the tribal communities through provision of infrastructural facilities, education, better healthcare and work /livelihood for economic development. Its impact can be seen from:
   o Disease free society with better hygiene and sanitation facilities
   o Improved sense of belonging towards community brought about with good educational programmes.

f. **Vanangana**: This NGO works towards the empowerment of women and protection of children within the tribal settlements. It empowers the women folk through various methods so that they and their children could be protected from discrimination. Its key programs are:
   o Providing legal and financial support to women and children who might be victims of violence and other forms of oppression
   o Skill development and education program for children

Section III:

SPECTACULAR REVIVAL OF VULNERABLE DOGRA CULTURE

Section deals with the history of Dogra rulers, the Dogra culture and the linguistic landscape in the complete State of J&K. Situations leading to decline of Dogra culture and the efforts of the govt. as well as the public that led to its spectacular revival are covered here.

Chapter 10: History of Dogra Rulers
Chapter 11: Rich and Pluralistic Dogra Culture
Chapter 12: Linguistic Landscape in J&K State and Decline of Dogri Language
Chapter 13: Revival of Dogri: Initiatives of Govt. & NGOs

HISTORY OF DOGRA RULERS

"Justice is my religion."

– Maharaja Hari Singh

The Jammu region of the State of Jammu and Kashmir, India, is often referred to as "Dogra Land" due to its rich heritage and cultural significance. It was predominantly ruled by Dogra kings for much of its history. Presently, the city of Jammu serves as the winter capital of Jammu & Kashmir.

Who are Dogras?

The Dogras are a very vibrant community, mainly residing in the Jammu region of J&K State, Himachal Pradesh, some parts of Pakistan and the neighboring areas. Their ancestors are believed to be that of the Indo-Aryan ethno-linguistic race which have been occupying the hills and plain areas in Northern India for thousands of years. The exact history of Dogras has been recreated by many researchers after studying old artifacts as well as the documents of those times.

Early History of Dogras

The Dogras, a prominent community from the Jammu region, have historically received limited coverage in the broader narrative of Indian history, largely due to their small and hilly kingdom. However, their rich heritage and lineage trace back to the Suryavanshi dynasty, the same dynasty in which Bhagwan Shree Ram was born in Ayodhya. The Dogras venerate Lord Ram as their family deity and identify themselves as Suryavanshis.

Earliest reference of Dogras has also been found when they fought wars with Alexander, the king of Macedon, a Greek kingdom, during 326-323 B.C. After Alexander crossed the Indus river, he had tough times fighting with kings like Porus and in the hill regions between rivers Beas and Jhelum. As per historians, he was killed by the Suryavanshi clan in the Rock citadel at Arnia (Salal), in the State of J&K.

An eleventh century old copper-plate inscription found in Chamba region of Himachal Pradesh, mentions a powerful kingdom *Durgara*, during medieval times, which was near to that region. The word *Durgara* is believed to have changed to *Duggar* over the times and people now call Dogra land as *Duggar Desh*. A few believe that the warriors who used to fight from their *Durg* (fort) and were fond of founding powerful kingdoms, came to be known as *Durg wala*, which later on got spelled as Dogras.

A 12th century poetic work Rajtrangini, written by Kalhana, a Kashmiri Pandit, mentions many places of Jammu region and their kings. He mentions Raja Vajradhara of Babbapura (Babor), a place 45 km from Jammu city. Babbapura is believed to be the earlier capital of *Duggar* kings before Jammu became capital much later.

History of Jammu

There is a folklore about the establishment of the city of Jammu, about 3,000 years ago when king Jambulochan, while on a hunting trip, found a goat and a lion drinking water together from the same pond. His religious guides explained that this soil was so virtuous that no living creature bore enmity against each other. This message impressed the king so much that he built his capital on this land which came out to be named after him as Jambupura which with the passage of time came to be known as Jammu.

Origin of Dogra Rulers of Jammu

The first name which figures in the history of Dogra land is Agnivir, the youngest son of Raja Sudershan who migrated to the areas around Kathua along river Ravi and ruled neighbouring villages including Kangra. Raja Sudershan, as per historical folklore, was the 20th descendant of *Bhagwan* Ram. That is why the recent Maharajas of J&K call themselves *Suryvanshies*. Agnivir's son, Raja Vayusharv ruled from a place near Kathua and extended his boundary up to river Ujh.

As per another folklore, Agnigarb whose forefather was Raja Vayusharv, was considered to be another influential Dogra ruler. He had two sons, Bahulochan and Jambulochan. Bahulochan had extended his boundary up to Bahu and started ruling from there. After his death, his younger brother Jambulochan became the next ruler who shifted his capital from Bahu to Jammu.

Rai Dynasty

In 50 BCE, the Rai Dynasty started ruling Jammu. It was founded by Adi Rai who is considered to be the first independent ruler of Jammu. He ruled for 40 years and after his death his son Dev Rai succeeded him, followed by 9 rulers like Gandharab Rai, Kadamb Rai, Karam Rai, Khir Rai, Khakhar Rai, Sind Rai, Jagat Rai, Dudh Rai and Jogi Rai.

Jogi Rai was the last ruler of this dynasty. Jogi Rai's elder son, Malhan Hans formed the Manhas clan and settled in Sialkot and his younger brother, Suraj Dhar founded the Dhar Dynasty in Jammu.

Dhar Dynasty (430-840 ADE)

Suraj Dhar established the Dhar dynasty in 430 ADE. He ruled for 55 years till 485. This dynasty ruled for 410 years till 840. Important rulers were Ganga Dhar, Devala Dhar, Sarkia Dhar, Kirat Dhar and Bajar Dhar. Other Dhar rulers included Raja Dharam Karan, Raja Kirat Karan, Raja Shakti Karan, Raja Sarpla Dhar, Raja Kirti Dhar, Raja Ajay Dhar and Raja Bijrala Dhar.

A Muslim saint Peer Roshan Shah Wali from Arab visited Jammu during the rule of this dynasty in the 7th century. His shrine is located at Gumat in Jammu city and is revered by all communities.

The last ruler of this dynasty was Bijarala Dhar after which Jammu was taken over by the Dev Dynasty.

Dev Dynasty (920-1780)

Jamwal Rajputs who were rulers of Duggar Pradesh find their lineage about 2,000 years ago and used to suffix 'Dhar' as their last name. It is only Raja Suraj Dev son of Raja Bijrala Dhar who ruled from 927 to 987 changed the surname from 'Dhar' to 'Dev'. Subsequently all his descendants used 'Dev' as their surname till 1688.

During this period, the capital of Jammu was Babbor (Babbarpura as mentioned in Rajatarangini) a place near Manwal on Udhampur-Dhar road. Notable rulers of Dev Density were:

- Raja Mal Dev
- Raja Hamir Dev
- Raja Bhiram Dev
- Maharaja Ranjit Dev

When the Mughal empire declined, Raja Ranjit Dev, who ascended the throne in 1733 CE became the independent ruler of Jammu. He constructed the famous Panjvakhtar Shiv Temple, the mosque at Mastgarth and Haveli Begum monuments at Jammu. He dominated 22 surrounding Hill states, with them becoming tributaries of Jammu. These included the then powerful states of Basolhi, Bhadarwah, Kishtwar and

Chanani. A very common local phrase that time was *"baayiyaan bich Jammu Sardar hai"*, meaning Jammu is chief of 22 hill states.

During Raja Kirapal's time, the Centre for Pahari Paintings at Basohli School flourished whereas Peer Kho cave temple of Lord Shiva was constructed at Jammu by Raja Ajeo Dev in 15th century.

Names of rulers/Jagirdars of Dev Dynasty are given at Table 10.1.

Rulers During 1780-1820

The downfall of the Mughals created a power vacuum. This is the time when Sikh Misls came to power in the Punjab area which had repercussions on the Hill states. Towards the end of Ranjit Dev's rule, the Sikh clans of Punjab (misls) gained ascendancy, and Jammu began to be contested by the Bhangi, Kanhaiya and Sukerchakia misls. During around 1770 CE, the Bhangi misl attacked Jammu and forced Ranjit Dev to become a tributary. Other sources state that Ranjit Dev was able to successfully fend-off the Sikh attacks on Jammu that occurred.

Raja Ranjit Dev was succeeded by Raja Braj Dev who ruled up to 1787. In the meantime, Sikh leader Mahan Singh plundered Jammu and took a *loot* of Rs. two crore from Jammu. Jammu lost its supremacy when Raja Braj Dev was killed during the Sikh invasion on Jammu.

After his death, the state of Jammu was under Punjabi rule. Raja Braj Dev's infant son Raja Sampuran Dev succeeded with Jammu becoming an autonomous tributary under Sikh rule. He was declared as a feudal lord to work under the control of his uncle Mian Mots. He died at the age of eleven years with no issue. His rule came to an end in 1797.

Sampuran Singh was succeeded by Raja Jit Singh, son of Dalel Singh. In a conflict with the Sikh empire, he lost and was exiled into British territory. With Jammu fully annexed by the Sikhs by around 1812. (1808 as per some historians), it remained under the direct rule of Sikh empire till 1820.

Table: 10.1: Dogra Rulers (Dev Dynasty) from 900 to 1780 ADE

S.No.	Period	Name of Ruler / Jagirdar
1.	900-920	Raja Bijrala Dhar
2.	920-987	Raja Surya Dev
3.	987-989	Raja Bhuj Dev
4.	989-1033	Raja Avtar Dev
5.	1033-1063	Raja Jas Dev
6.	1063-1094	Raja Sangram Dev
7.	1094-1164	Jaskara Dev
8.	1164-1215	Braj Dev
9.	1215-1245	Narsingh Dev
10.	1245-1312	Arjan Dev
11.	1312-1359	Jodha Dev
12.	1359-1399	Mal Dev
13.	1399-1423	Bhim Dev or Hamir Dev
14.	1423-1454	Ajab Dev
15.	1454-1500	Bikram Dev
16.	1500-1530	Khokhar Dev
17.	1530-1571	Kapoor Dev
18.	1571-1596	Sambhal Dev
19.	1596-1626	Sangram Dev
20.	1526-1552	Bhupat Dev
21.	1652-1688	Hari Dev
22.	1688-1703	Gajey Singh
23.	1703-1742	Dhruv Dev
24.	1742-1780	Ranjit Dev. As per some other sources, it was during 1733-1783 CE.

Contribution of Raja Gulab Singh till 1822

In 1820, Raja Kishore Singh, who was great grandson of Raja Dharab Singh and grandson of Surat Singh, became Raja of Jammu. After his death in 1822, his son Raja Gulab Singh became Raja of Jammu.

Gulab Singh, during his childhood was trained in war tactics by his grandfather Zorawar Singh. Later he joined the services of Maharaja

Ranjit Singh at Lahore Durbar. Within a few years of his recruitment, he led many campaigns for Maharaja Ranjit Singh and played a key role in the consolidation and the management of the Sikh kingdom.

As a military commander, he led many campaigns including the following:

- Siege of Kashmir in 1812
- Conquest of Jalandhar
- Conquest of Reasi in 1815-16
- Frontier campaigns between 1815-19
- Conquest of Multan in 1819
- Conquest of Kishtwar and Rajouri in 1821

Mian Dido Jamwal, who was leading a rebellion against the Sikhs was captured and executed by him. He had become one of the most powerful chiefs of Sikh empire and was entitled to keep a personal army of 3 infantry regiments, 15 artillery guns and 40 garrison guns.

Gulab Singh earned the title of "Jewal in the Lahore Durbar".

Raj-Tilak Ceremony of Raja Gulab Singh

The title of Raja was bestowed on Gulab Singh by Maharaja Ranjit Singh, the then ruler of Punjab. On June 17, 1822, he came to the Jammu region and applied the *tilk* on the forehead of Raja Gulab Singh. This ceremony was performed at Jia Pota tree on the bank of Chenab at Akhnoor. The direct rule of the latest generation of Dogras in Jammu commenced.

His expansion spree continued. In 1824 he captured the fort of Samartah near Mansar Lake. In 1827, he accompanied Sikh Commander-in-Chief Hari Singh Nalwa and defeated Afghan rebels in the battle of Shaidu, currently in Khyber Pakhtunistan, Pakistan.

Under the Treaty of Amritsar on 16 March 1846 between the British East India Company and Raja Gulab Singh, Jammu and Kashmir was purchased by Raja Gulab Singh who became Maharaja of Jammu and Kashmir in 1946.

As far as Kashmir is concerned, it was annexed by Mughals under Akbar in 1586. From then till 1752, it was under the Mughal empire after which the Durani empire started off till 1819 with the exception of 8 years from 1754 to 1762 when Raja Jiwan was the king of Kashmir. From Durranis, the Sikh empire took over control of Kashmir from 1819 to 1846.

Rulers of Jammu and Kashmir (1846 to 1925)

Maharaja Gulab Singh was the first king of unified Jammu and Kashmir. He consolidated the complete state after 1846. He also allowed the Sikh soldiers to join their brethren in Punjab in the Second Sikh War in 1849. The fort of Chilas in the Dard country was conquered by him in 1850. It is the largest area which lies astride the Indus River and Naga Parbat. Its inhabitants were Baltis, Bhutte and Dard. He handed over the reigns of J&K to his son Ranbir Singh in 1856.

Maharaja Ranjit Singh, during his tenure, consolidated the state and expanded its borders by annexing Gilgit and incorporating Hunza and Nagar into the state. He was also a scholar of Sanskrit and Persian. He established a modern judicial system and compiled civil and criminal laws into the Ranbir Penal Code. These laws were being followed till August 2019. He founded separate departments for foreign affairs, home affairs and the army. Founded a silk factory in Jammu and promoted the shawl industry.

He modified Dogri to make it compatible for lithe printing and called the new language as *Namme Dogra Akkhar*. He also established a *Sanskrit Pathshala in* the complex of Raghunath temple at Jammu. He built roads even in hilly areas.

On his death, on 12 September 1885, his son Pratap Singh succeeded him as Maharaja of J&K. Maharaja Pratap Singh ruled the state for 40 years from 1885 to 1925, the longest of all the Dogra rulers.

He improved infrastructure in a big way. Made Jhelum Valley Cart Road from Kohala to Baramulla, the most beautiful mountain road in the world and next year extended it to Srinagar. Also made roads from

Srinagar to Gilgit in Baltistan and Leh in Ladakh. He developed the river Jhelum as an important means of transportation. In 1922, another great highway, the Banihal Cart Road was completed and inaugurated. This Cart Road connected Srinagar, the summer capital, with Jammu, the winter capital of the state.

He developed Jammu and constructed the Tawi bridge and Jammu-Sialkot railway line. He had also made plans to connect Jammu with Srinagar via rail line, but this could not fructify.

He popularized education by opening many schools for boys and girls. Education in the primary classes was made free. Encouraged education in the poor populace of Muslim community also. He started a degree college named Prince of Wales College (now named GGM Science College) in Jammu in 1905 and another degree college named Sri Pratap College at Srinagar in 1907.

Similarly, for providing medical facilities to the citizens, he opened many hospitals for all.

As a result of the performance of Dogra soldiers during the First World War, he was granted new imperial honors and a 21-gun salute in place of 19-gun salute.

Rule of Maharaja Hari Singh (1925-1947)

Maharaja Pratap Singh, at the time of his death, had no surviving issue. So, the reigns of Jammu and Kashmir came into the hands of Hari Singh, nephew of Maharaja Pratap Singh and son of Raja Amar Singh. He became Maharaja of J&K in 1925.

He got his education in Mayo College in Ajmer, India at the age of 13 years. Later he went to Imperial Cadets Corps at Dehradun (currently Indian Military Academy (IMA)) for his military training. In 1915, Maharaja Pratap Singh appointed him Commander-in-Chief of the State Forces.

He formed *Praja Sabha* and conducted elections in the state for the first time. To discuss the political future of India, he was invited to the First Round Table Conference in London.

In 1932, Sheikh Abdullah, great grandson of a Hindu Brahmin of the Sapru clan (as per his autobiography Aatish-e-Chinar), formed the Kashmir Muslim Conference in 1932 and became its President. In 1946, he launched Quit Kashmir agitation against Maharaja Hari Singh and was arrested but later released on 29 September 1947.

In 1947, when India got independence, J&K decided to remain as an independent country. But soon after partition of India, the tribal people supported by the army of the newly formed Pakistan attacked Jammu & Kashmir with the aim to annex J&K. Then he approached the Indian govt. for help, signed the Instrument of Accession and joined India as one of the Indian states on 26 Oct 1947. But by that time Pakistan had captured one third of Jammu and Kashmir to which India refers as Pakistan-occupied-Jammu Kashmir (POJK) whereas Pakistan calls it Azad Kashmir.

Later, on 20 June 1949, Maharaja Hari Singh left J&K and went to Bombay where he spent his life till his death in 1961, as a normal citizen of India.

J&K after 1947

On merger with India, Sheikh Abdullah was appointed Head of the Emergency Administration of J&K on 30 October 1947 and later became Prime Minister of J&K in March 1948. Karan Singh, son of Maharaja Hari Singh, was appointed as Prince Regent of J&K in 1949, at the age of just 18 years.

Later in 1953, Sheikh Abdullah was dismissed as Prime Minister of J&K by the then Sadr-i-Riyasat Dr. Karan Singh, son of Maharaja Hari Singh. The then Home Minister of J&K, Bakshi Ghulam Mohd. became Prime Minister of J&K.

End of Dogra Rule

After 26 Oct 1947, Dogra rule ended in J&K, and it became one of the 14 states of India which declared itself as a secular democratic country. India became a Republic and adopted the newly approved Constitution on 26 January 1950 which provides for a parliamentary form of government.

Prominent Dogra Personalities

- Banda Singh Bahadur, Commander of Khalsa Army, a Sikh warrior, popularly called Band Bir Bahadur
- Pt. Shiv Kumar Sharma, classical music and Santoor player
- Zakir Hussain, Indian Tabla Player and composer
- Major Somnath, a Dogra officer, the first Param Vir Chakra Awardee in India.

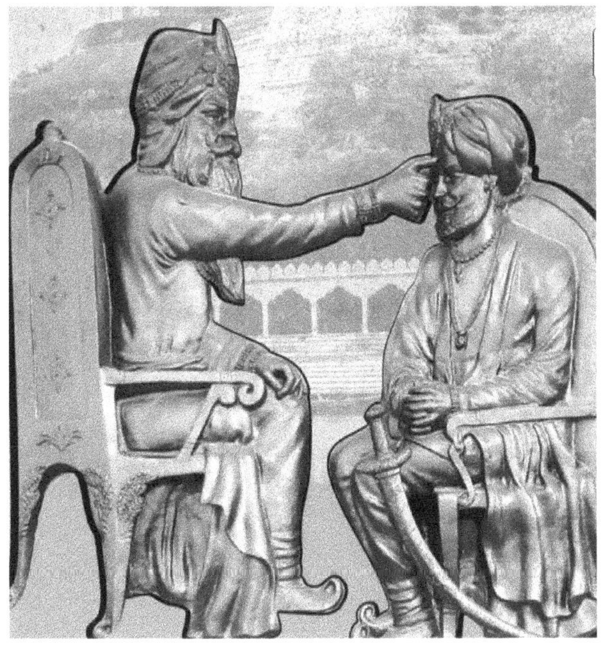

Fig 10.1: Raj Tilk of Raja Gulab Singh by Maharaja Ranjit Singh, Maharaja of Punjab at Jia Pota, Akhnoor, J&K on 17 June 1822

Family Tree of Rajas/Maharajas of Jammu

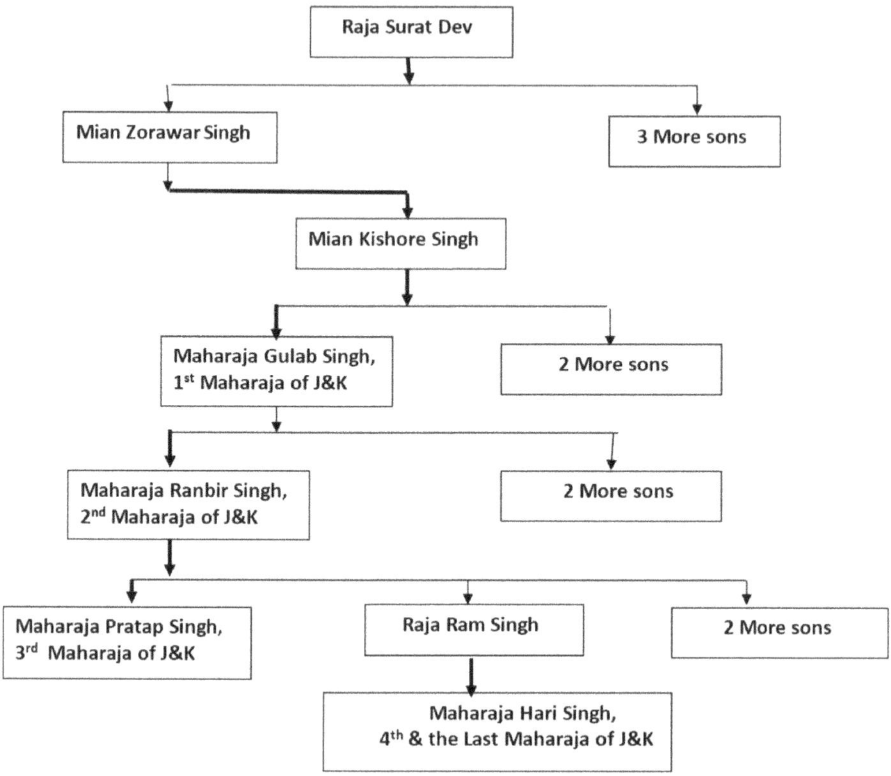

Fig 10.2: Family tree of Rajas and Maharajas at J&K

Maharajas of Jammu & Kashmir
(1846-1947)

Maharaja Gulab Singh
1846-1856

Maharaja Ranbir Singh
1856-1885

Maharaja Pratap Singh
1885-1925

Maharaja Hari Singh
1925-1947

Fig 10.3: Maharajas of J&K from 1846 to 1947

Chapter 11

RICH AND PLURALISTIC DOGRA CULTURE

Mithhdi ai Dogrein di boli te khand mithe lok Dogre
(Dogri language is very sweet, and the Dogra people are as sweet as sugar)

A common Dogri couplet

Dogra culture is a secular culture comprising people belonging to different religions, tribes and castes in the areas of Jammu, Himachal Pradesh, some parts of Punjab in India and the adjoining areas of Sialkot in Pakistan. The people staying here are known as Dogras, and the region is popularly known as *Duggar Desh* or Dogra land. Their mother tongue is *Dogri* and the script is *Takri*. However, under the influence of dominant scripts, *Takri* has become almost extinct, and locals have switched over to *Devnagari* as its script.

In this chapter, glimpses of Dogra culture in terms of its family system, festivals, fairs, heritage places, rituals, salutation method, cuisine and dresses etc. will be covered.

Family System

In the olden days, Dogras used to follow a joint family system where one can see the grandparents, parents and children staying under the same roof. In some families, even the uncles and their children stay next-door. The number of members in some of the typical families could be 15 to 25 on average. All stay peacefully and everyone obeys the orders of the eldest in the family without any argument.

However, nowadays, things have changed, though this type of joint family living can still be seen in the rural areas and villages. In the present scenario, as the children had to move out to different cities for jobs/ business, the structure of joint families is breaking. Still the bonding among the family members is very strong.

Temperament of Dogras

Dogras are a martial race capable of fighting guerrilla warfare as well as frontal fights in high mountains of the Himalayas. The icons are Mian Dido of Nagrota, who undertook guerrilla tactics for years together to save his people from the atrocities of the outsides. Their second icon is General Zorawar Singh, who conquered Leh, Ladakh besides certain territories in the present Pakistan occupied Jammu & Kashmir (POJK). He had gone up to Tibet to conquer it but had to stop the battle due to unavoidable reasons. All the Dogras feel proud of their having marshal character.

Dogri Couplet

As Dogre han, aakhne aan shaan kane.
Assen jangaan jitiyan n ghamsaan kanne
(Translation: We feel proud to call ourselves as Dogras.
We have won wars purely on our muscle power)

By profession, they are agriculturists, businessmen and have a craze to serve the nation by joining the Indian Armed Forces. Otherwise, Dogras are known to be fun loving and cool people. They care for each other and consider a guest as an incarnation of God. Their hospitable nature is worth praising. However, they do not tolerate nonsense and whenever it comes to their prestige, their natural martial-like qualities become visible, and they have the capability to thrash out the opponent. Their character is well summarized in a Dogri poem (Fig. 11.1), English translation of which is also given along with it.

**Character of Dogras
Explained in a Dogri Poem**

खंड बी डोगरे, खीर बी डोगरे,

खुये दा ठंडा, नीर बी डोगरे,

आकड़े कोई ते, पीर बी डोगरे,

डंडे दी गल्ल समझाई जायां,

डोगरा देस जगाई जायां

English Translation

Dogras are as sweet as sugar,

they are like sweet dish

Dogras are as cool as water from a deep well

If someone shows them force,

then they are capable of thrashing him

Convey them the language of stick

Waken up the Dogra Community

Fig. 11.1: Dogri poem indicating character of Dogras

Dogra Rituals

Most of the Dogras are Hindu by religion. They perform 16 ceremonies from birth till death. However, a few of these will be explained here.

1. *Reetan and Sutra*: This is the ceremony which is performed when a woman gets pregnant for the first time. Then in the 8th month of her pregnancy the woman wears yellow or red clothes and is asked to sit on a special seat called *Peeda* in local parlance. Then she is given some coconuts, almonds and other dry fruits as a sign of God's blessings. Parents of the woman bring food which is distributed and eaten by all present.

   In the ninth month of pregnancy, sweet dish *Sund* which is rich in dry fruits, is given to her for consumption during the month so that she bears a healthy child. After the child is born, the naming of the child is done on the 11th, 13th, 16th or 21st day, based on the sex and caste of the baby. The name of the newborn is suggested by *Buya*, the sister-in-law of the mother. This ceremony is called *Sutra*.

2. Pre-Marriage Functions: Many functions called *Roka, Thhaka, Tikka/Sagan, Gandian* are performed before the actual marriage, primarily to select the partner till performance of the ring ceremony which is generally one or two days prior to the main marriage. A red thread by *Purohit*, the religious preacher, is tied on the right wrist of the girl or the boy that indicates a binding on them for not going out of the house till completion of the marriage.

3. *Saant*: On the day of the marriage or a day before that, a ceremony of holy bath is performed by the boy/girl. In the case of the bride, *Mama*, the maternal uncle gives her some gifts, lifts her and takes her up to the place where the marriage ceremony is performed by *Pundit ji*. This ceremony is known as *Saant* and special traditional food made that day is called *Santti da Patt*. A small wooden structure called *Tooran* is made and tied at the entrance

of the house. A special musical instrument *Kail*, a 6-feet long folding trumpet, is blown by the barber of that area indicating the beginning of the *Saant*.

4. On Marriage Day: On that day, the bridegroom with face covered by small strings and riding a decorated mare, goes to the bride's place in a procession. He is nicely attired and holds a sword in his hand as a tradition depicting him as part of the martial race. He is accompanied by his relatives and friends (called *baratees*) in a procession. This procession is known as *Jaani* which is preceded by a musical band which makes everyone dance to the vibrant and energetic tunes of the latest local songs. On reaching the bride's house, the *Jaani* is served with a good traditional dinner. Friends and relatives from both sides are witness to it and enjoy the delicious meals. After dispersal, sometime during midnight, at an auspicious time announced by the *Pandit ji*, the final marriage ceremony is performed around a campfire where the bride and the bridegroom take seven rounds around the fire amidst chanting of the hymns by the religious *Purohits* of both the sides. This activity is called *Saat Ferre* or *Lamma Ferre*.

Like the rituals during birth and marriages, there are many rituals for occasions including at the time of the demise of someone in the family.

Greetings and Salutation: Dogras have a unique system of greeting each other. It is very common for Hindus using the words like *Bhaiyaa/papa/pra ji* for elder brother and *didi/bobo/bhainji* for sisters. However, in offices, they may use English words like Sir, Madam etc. Muslims use the words like *Janab, Mohtarma, asslamalekum, valekumsalaam* etc. whereas the Sikhs use the word *Sat Shri Akal*.

The salutation is different within different castes of Hindus. When a Rajput meets another Rajput, they greet each other by the word *Jai Deva* whereas when a younger Brahmin meets another elder Brahmin, he/she greets the elders by the words *Charanbandna* or *Peri Pauna* (meaning that I take your blessing by touching your feet). Elderly persons reciprocate the younger ones by saying *Jinda ro, Lammi Umran hon,* whereas to the married ladies, they say *Bud suhagin ho* or *sat putri ho.*

However, in urban areas people have started using the common Hindi word *Namaste* and, in the offices, they use English words like good morning, good evening etc.

Professional Choice of Locals

Most of the Dogras staying in the villages are petty farmers besides a few small businesspeople. The land of the region is called *Kandi ka Ilaqa.* meaning semi barren land which needs a lot of effort to grow the crop. So, in the hilly areas, crop produce is very little.

Dogras, being a martial race, have a natural inkling towards joining defence forces. In the Indian Army, there are three regiments where a sizable number of troops are Dogras. These regiments are DOGRA Regiment, Jammu and Kashmir Rifles (JAK Rif) and Jammu and Kashmir Light Infantry (JAK LI). There are many Dogras who have been Generals/ Lt. Generals/ Major Generals in the Indian Army. General Nirmal Chander Vij has even risen to the highest rank in the Army and was the Chief of the Army Staff to command around 1.3 million soldiers of the country.

When the State of J&K was under British rule, it had taken part in both the World Wars and fought adversaries of the British Army on all the fronts of East Asia, Europe, North Africa including the much talked of Burma Campaign on the Eastern side. Chivalry of the troops could be seen from the number of gallantry awards bestowed on them by the British Army. The Dogra Regiment got two Victoria Crosses, the highest and most prestigious decoration in the British Armed Forces, 44 Military crosses and many other awards from them.

Besides the above, in the urban areas one can find many locals such as businesspeople, artisans, house workers, engineers, doctors etc.

Prominent Fairs and Festivals among the Dogras

Fairs and festivals are an integral part of Dogra culture. These are innumerable and are equally varied in origin marking the local, religious, seasonal and social fervor. Many of these are dedicated to various deities, saints and prophets. Each festival is unique in style and is characterized by colour, gaiety, enthusiasm, feasts and rituals. Many national festivals have also been adopted by the Dogras in their own way.

The message of love and brotherhood among various religions and communities can be seen when all of them join in the festivals and fairs, and celebrate together, on big fairgrounds or the religious places. These festivals besides uniting the communities also serve many other purposes like employment generation, entertainment, shopping, pilgrimage etc. In the words of Yogi Adityanath, Chief Minister of Uttar Pradesh, India, the financial impact of a cultural event is:

The festival of Mahakumb of 2025 at Prayagraj would generate income worth 10% of GDP (Gross Domestic Product) of the State.

Some of the prominent festivals are explained here in brief.

1. **Lohri:** This festival falls on the *Makar Sankranti* day, the 13th of January, every year and heralds the onset of spring when the whole of Jammu region wears a festive look. It is dedicated to the Gods of Sun and Fire. It is more of a social festival than a religious one. Young boys prepare *Chhajja* from bamboo sticks, decorate it with colored paper and perform *Chhajja* dance on the beats of *dhol*, local drums. They move from house to house in the streets, dance and sing songs and finally ask for gifts. All those who give good gifts or money, the singing group generally shout *Dabba Bhariya leeran da, Ei Kar amirran Da,* meaning that the house is of rich people. And those who do not give befitting gifts, the singing party shouts *Hukka bhai hukka, ai kaar bhukha,* meaning that this house is of miser people.

Like the boys, the girls also form their groups and go from one house to another asking for gifts by singing local songs. Even the small children form groups and go to the houses rattling the common popular Dogri poem, given below.

Sunder mundriye O, Tera kaun Bechara O,
Dulla Bhatti wala O, Dule Dhi Bihayee O,
Ser Shakkar payee O, Kudi da salu pata, O

2. ***Thagren da Vart:*** A prominent Hindu festival *Janmashtami* is celebrated all over the country to mark the birth of Lord Krishna. In the Jammu region, it is popularly called *Thagren da vart* (meaning fast dedicated to Thakur i.e. Shri Krishna). It falls on the Eighth day of the *Krishna Paksha* in the month of *Bhadrapada*. On that day most of the temples are suitably decorated, beautifully lit and are a great attraction for the devotees. Recitation of *mantras* in the temples, playing dramas enacting the life of Shri Krishan are some of the activities in the temples.

In Jammu, the main attraction is the Raghunath temple at which a *shobha yatra* (a procession of devotees), culminates. At midnight, exactly at 12 O' clock, the birth of Shri Krishna is depicted by removing a curtain from the *Ball Roop* (infant shape) of Shri Krishan, who is shown in a crawling pose in a pram or a swing. Amidst chanting of the *mantras*, people swing the *Ball roop* of Shri Krishan to take His blessings.

Other main activities are:

- ○ Observing fast throughout the day by everyone in the house. Some keep *Phallahari Vrat* i.e. they are permitted to eat fruit or preparations of fruits only whereas others keep normal *vrat* where people eat special items like *siyool, bajarbhang, aloo ki tikki*, curd and bread made of *Dhraion ka atta.*
- ○ Kites are flown by all the communities, which is the main attraction of the day. And everyone enjoys that. One can find people on their rooftops, flying kites of different colors and sizes.

On some roofs, one can find the big gatherings which play songs on DJ and dance as and when any kite is snapped by them. This event is joined by the people of all the religions.

3. **Baisakhi:** It is a harvest festival and falls on the 1st of *Baisakh* (first day of the month *Baisakh*) every year. This festival has a special significance for the Sikh community as the Khalsa religion was established on this day by the tenth Guru viz. Guru Gobind Singh ji in 1699. They celebrate it all over the world and Dogras also attach significance to it.

    On this day many cultural programmes are organized in all the cities and towns of Jammu. Large fairs are organized preceded by vibrant processions showcasing traditional attire, folk music and dance performances. *Bhangra* and colourful *Gidda* are the most famous among all the dances. In all the gurudwaras, there are *bhajans, keertans* and *lungar seva* for all. Gurudwara Bibi Chand Kaur at Jammu and Shiromani Dera Nangali Sahib at Poonch are the two biggest gurudwaras in Jammu region. Prayers start in the morning and culminate by mid noon after which *prasad* is served to all.

    In *Lungar*, the community kitchen, free food service is available to all irrespective of caste, creed and religion. This promotes values of equality, humility and community service.

4. ***Navratras:*** *Navratri* is a special festival celebrated all over the country and is very famous for the Dogra community too. The literal meaning of *Navratri* is nine nights. These nine days are solely dedicated to Durga Mata and her nine *avtars* i.e. incarnations. The first day is devoted to Mata Shailaputri, second to Mata Brahmcharini and similarly the last day is for Mata Siddidatri. Each *avtar* of Mata Vaishno Devi gives us special strength and fulfills our wishes.

    Culturally, these festivals are dedicated to Goddess Durga, an exemplar of *Shakti*, the cosmic energy, and is believed to accord spiritual and worldly fulfilment. *Navratras* are celebrated twice a year for nine days each time. *Navratras* which fall during winter months are known as *Shardiya Navratras* and those falling in summer months are called *Chaitra Navratras.*

Mata Vaishno Devi is considered as the deity of Jammu, and her main temple is at Trikuta hills in Katra town where celebrations are immense. Energetic gatherings can also be seen at The Kali temple, Bahu Fort Jammu during these *Navratras.*

○ ***Navratri* at Mata Vaishno Devi, Bhawan Katra:** This temple is very famous across India. Though pilgrims keep visiting it throughout the year, it has special significance during *Navratras.* Decorations at this place are of very high order and *bhajan, keetans, havans,* etc. are done methodically. Discourse on the life of each of the *Avtars* of Mata Vaishno Devi is given by some prominent personality, each day during *Navratras.*

○ **Bawe Wali Mata, Jammu:** This is the temple of Goddess Kali Mata at Bahu Fort in Jammu city itself. Locals have a great faith in this temple, and they believe that during the wars between India and Pakistan in 1965 and 1971, Jammu was saved by its deity and that is why not even a single bomb shell landed here even during the immense air attack by Pakistan.

Especially on *Naratras,* the devotees throng it throughout the day from early in the morning till late night. Thousands of devotees could be seen standing in a long queue in front of the temple at any time of the day. Havan is continuously performed here and *lungar seva* is organized almost throughout the day on all these days.

5. **Festival of Bhagwan Shiv:** Dogras also believe in *Shaivism* and worship Bhagwan Shiv on almost all the occasions. His temples are found in complete Dogra land and people worship Him on an almost daily basis. As per Hindu mythology, Bhawan Shiv is believed to have saved the world from destruction by consuming the poison which came out during *Samudra Manthan,* a churning process of the sea.

A special day of Bhagwan Shiv is Maha Shiv Ratri "the Great Night of Shiva" or the marriage anniversary day when Bhagwan Shiv tied the nuptial knot with Mata Parvati. As per Sadguru, Founder of Isha Foundation:

"Mahashivratri is of great significance for all those who aspire for the Ultimate. May this night become an exuberant awakening for you"

It is a common belief in Dogra land that the desires of all those who worship Bhagwan Shiv are fulfilled very fast. Monday, the first day of the week, is dedicated to Bhagwan Shiv. All those who keep fast for 16 Mondays continuously will be the blessed ones and on whom Bhagwan Shiv will shower His blessings and bring happiness to their families.

Shiv Tandav Nritya, the cosmic dance done by Bhawan Shiv, is very famous. This dance form is very energetic and explained beautifully, as a sacred hymn *Shiv Tandav Stotram* by Ravan, the king of Lanka. It is for everyone's spiritual growth and self-improvement. It is believed that the chanting of this *Stotra* calms the mind, removes obstacles from life, gives mental strength, removes negative vibes and gives divine blessings. Main Shiv temples in the Dogra land are:

- Shiv Khori at Reasi: In this temple over six hundred thousand pilgrims visited and paid their abeyance on the *Shiv Raatri* of 2024
- Purmandal: It is a place around 25 km from Jammu, on the bank of the River Devika, also called Gupta Ganga. This place is also known as *Chhota Kashi*. It is home to many *Shiv Lings* which are believed to have originated naturally at this place. Main temple is known as Umapati temple. During *Shiv Ratri*, the festivities last for 3 days.
- Sudh Maha Dev: A 3-day festival is held during June-July on the full moon night of the month of *Sawan* to worship *Trident* (Trishul and a mace.). Cultural programmes are organized during these three days in which local performers entertain the visitors by showcasing various local dances and singing folk songs.

- ○ Peer Kho or Jamwant Gufa at Jammu: It is again a Shiv cave-temple on the bank of River Tawi which is thronged by devotees on Shiv Ratri day.
- ○ Ranbireshwar and Panjvaktra Temples at Jammu: At both these temples, the devotees organize many *lungers* too.

A unique community of devotees of Bhagwan Shiv, popularly known as *Jangams*, is famous in Jammu who recite *Shiv Vivah* very elaborately. *Jangams* are believed to be the descendants of those devotees who had witnessed the marriage of Bhagwan Shiv. They are differently attired and can be recognized from a far-off distance.

6. ***Jagranas***: Night-long discourses of religious *bhajans*, known as *Jagranas* start at about 8 pm in the night, continue throughout the night and culminate by morning. *Jagranas* for Mata Vaishno Devi and Machhail Mata are very common. In addition to this, there are *Akhand Paths* like *Ramayan Akhand Path* which are for 24-, 36- or 48-hours duration.

   Hanuman Chalisa, Sunder Kand etc. are one-hour long programmes and are enchanted by smaller groups on weekly or monthly basis. Generally, Tuesdays are earmarked for *Hanuman Chalisa* or *Durga Puja*.

7. **Community Melas:** Besides common festivals and fairs, there are a few fairs or gatherings which are specific to certain communities and in local parlance are called *Mel or Mela*. Members of a particular community meet at least once a year at their *Devsthan*. These *Mels* are generally held during the winter months.

   Gagged in multicolored dresses, one can see the enthusiasm in the people when they participate actively in these *Mels*. Many a times, it is seen that people from other communities also join in these *Mels* thus showing the togetherness in society. Prominent *Mels/Melas* are covered here.

o **Jhiri Mela**: It is held on *Kartik Purnima* which falls during October-November every year. Celebrations are held at Jhiri village, around 20 km from Jammu on the Jammu-Akhnoor highway. Mela is celebrated to commemorate the martyrdom of Baba Jittoo, a simple honest farmer, who gave up his life against the oppressive demands of a landlord about 500 years ago. He preferred to take the extreme step of ending his life over the burning heap of wheat crop rather than yielding to the unjust demands.

  Millions of devotees, from all parts of India who have their ancestral links with Jhiri village come here annually to participate in it.

o **Chamliyal Mala**: A unique example of brotherhood among the border villages of India and Pakistan can be seen at the village Chamliyal, 40 km from Jammu. As the story goes, around 320 years ago, Baba Dalip Singh Manhas, a local saint, who had miraculous healing powers against skin diseases used to stay there. One day, when he was riding a horse and going to visit Saidanvali village (now in Pakistan), he was murdered by some miscreants. His head fell on the same spot in that village, but the horse ran back and brought his body to Chamliyal village. Since then, people of both the villages have been celebrating this event in their own villages, which falls on the fourth Thursday of June every year.

  Residents of Saidanwali are permitted to cross the Indo-Pak border that day up to Chamliyal Village. They bring with them a *chaddar* for the Shrine of Baba Chamliyal. In return, they take from here holy "*Shakkar*" (clay) and "*Sharbat*" (sweet water) back to their village. It is believed that this *Shakkar* and *Sharbat* are blessed and have great medicinal properties against various skin ailments.

  The fair is for three days at both the villages in Pakistan as well in India, where a lot many cultural events are organized by the respective governments.

- ○ ***Biradari Mels***: There are many other *Mels* celebrated by specific communities, where thousands of community members participate. During these *Mels*, routine *puja of Kul Devta or Kul Devi* (family deity) is done amidst chanting of *mantras* by a *pundit*. Generally, *Havan, Puran Ahuti* and *Pujan* are performed followed by *Preeti bhoj* (community lunch) by all. A few of these *Biradari Mels* are as below:

  - ➢ *Magotra Biradari Mel* at the premises of *Bua Rani* temple at Chowadi, Jammu
  - ➢ *Khajuria Biradari Mel* at *Dev Sthan, Baba Ambo*, near Bagh-e-Bahu, Jammu
  - ➢ *Katal Rajput Biradari* at *Kuldev Sthan*, Katli, Samba
  - ➢ *Jasrotia Biradari Mel* at Village Jasrota
  - ➢ *Boparai and Dalal Biradari* at their *Devsthan* in Langrial, RS Pura
  - ➢ *Sudan Brahmin Community* at *Bawa Satto Sidh* Ji Temple, Jandial

8. **Festivals/ Fasts for specific wishes**: There are many important days which are celebrated mainly by the ladies for specific wishes. A few of these are:

   - ○ **Karwa Chauth**: It is a Hindu festival that symbolizes love and devotion between the married couples. On this day, the married women fast from sunrise to moonrise and pray for the good health and long life of their husbands. During this period, they do not drink even a drop of water. They are also prohibited from undertaking any stitching work as it is believed that, by doing that, the husband will get pricks of the needle used for the work.

   - ○ ***Pugga Vrat***: This fast is kept by the mothers for the well-being of their children and seek blessings for happiness, long life and protection from evil spirits.

   - ○ ***Bachh Dua***: This is also celebrated by women for the long life of their sons. Mothers keep fast the whole day, visit temples to perform rituals and pray for the long life and well-being of their sons. It reflects the strong cultural values of the Dogra community, highlighting motherhood and family ties.

o **Dhrupadi**: It is another Dogra festival like the *Bachh Dua* but falls on *Radha Ashtami*. A bunch of 16 specs of a typical grass *dhrub* is made to worship *Kul Devta*. Small children are also swirled by two ladies for their long life with a belief that *Kuldevta* will protect them from evil powers.

o **Rutt-Raade**: This festival is celebrated for the growth of the family and promotes the welfare of the community. The unmarried girls plant seeds in the pitchers' necks, symbolizing family prosperity. Each pitcher, known as *Raada*, represents a brother whereas the large *Raada* represents the head of the family. These *Raadas* are carefully nurtured and decorated over a month after which these are immersed in water with proper rituals.

o **Tamdeh**: This festival falls in the month of June on the *Sankranti* day of the Hindu month of *Ashadh*. On this day, people take holy baths in rivers, offer fruits, flowers, pitchers/vessels filled with water, do charity and worship for the peace of the souls of their ancestors.

o **Shraadh**: The male Hindus remember their deceased ancestors on their death anniversary and do charity on a specific day during a 15-day period during September-October every year. It is a system of honoring and paying homage to the deceased ancestors.

Only a glimpse of a few of the festivals have been given here. However, besides above, there are many more festivals like *Ram Navmi, Gurupurav, Eid, Xmas, Budh Purnima*, etc. which are also celebrated on the Dogra land. National and State days like 26 January (Republic Day), 15th August (Independence Day), 2nd October (Gandhi Jayanti), 26th October (Vilay Diwas) etc. are also celebrated with pomp and show.

In cities, some of the above festivals have surrendered to modernization and are becoming extinct whereas these are still celebrated with full enthusiasm in the rural Duggar land and the traditional Duggar families.

Dogra Heritage Places

Dogra culture, being a very old culture, has its heritage monuments and religious places at many locations. However, a few of these, given below, are worth visiting/paying obeisance in case one plans a visit to Duggar land:

- Shri Mata Vaishno Devi Shrine: Visited by over 10 million pilgrims every year
- Raghunath Temple Jammu: Biggest temple in Jammu city
- Sudh Mahadev and Mantalai, Udhampur: Highly revered Shiv temples
- Krimchi Temples in Udhampur district
- Sukrala Mata and Mata Sundri temples in Kathua district
- Gurudwara Singh Sabha, Kathua
- Machail Chandi Mata and Vasukinag Temples at Doda-Kishtwar-Bhaderwah
- Ziarat Zain Shah Sahib, Doda
- Baba Budhan Ali Shah Dargah: Most famous Durgah at Jammu
- Maharani Chand Kaur Gurudwara: Biggest Gurudwara in Jammu
- Mubarak Mandi Jammu: It is the royal residence of Maharajas of Jammu & Kashmir
- Amar Mahal Palace, Jammu: Region's rich history and cultural heritage can be seen here
- Dogra Art Museum, Jammu: Repository of Dogra cultural heritage
- Bahu fort, Jammu: A historic fort in Jammu city
- Bhim Garh fort, Reasi: Built by famous Dogra General Zorawar Singh
- Ramnagar Fort, Udhampur district

Typical Dogra Dresses

With modernization creeping in, dresses all over the world are becoming standardized. Gents wear pants and shirts. However, the dress of ladies depends on the region they belong to. Same is the case with Dogras. However, the Dogras staying in rural areas still wear traditional dress whereas in functions in urban areas, few of the traditional families also wear the traditional dress. Traditional dresses for gents and ladies are given below:

- Traditional Dress for Dogra Gents
  - Long *Kurta (shirt)*
  - *Ghattnna*, (a churidar tight pajama)
  - *Saafa* (Turban)
  - And a half coat or long coat

- Traditional Dress for Dogra Ladies
  - *Kamiz* (long shirt)
  - *Sutthan.* A trouser known as Dogri *sutthan* is loose at the top but very tight from the knees to the ankles. There are also many pleats near the ankle.
  - *Dupatta:* It is a long scarf thrown over the shoulders and sometimes used to cover the face from elders known as *jhundd kadna.* The borders of scarves are decorated with *zari* and *kinari* to give a festive look to these.
  - *Kamiz* and *Chuni* are made attractive by stitching pearls, *kinari, zari* and many other shining materials on their borders.
  - Jewelry for Dogra Ladies: Every Indian woman irrespective of socio-economic standing would like to wear jewels of her choice. Even during marriages, jewelry is given as a wedding gift, as a symbol of commitment and even as a sign of the place they belong. The following items are very popular:
    - ➤ *Kanthis* around their neck
    - ➤ *Gokhrus and bangaan* on the hands

> *Jumkas and balis* on the ears
> *Ring* on the fingers
> *Nupura:* a large anklet
> *Nath* or nose ring has a special significance and is a sign of married ladies

Due to its uniqueness, the Dogri jewelry, especially the Dogri *Jhumkas*, have gained popularity across the country and can be seen in many jewelry stores.

Dogra Cuisine Choice

Dogras are fond of spicy as well as sweet food items. Their traditional food items vary from location to location depending upon the local produce of that area. However, their daily platter would contain at least one of the following items:

- *Rajmash* (a special variety of red kidney beans)
- *Chane/Rongi ki dal* (gram and small beans)
- *Kulth di daal* (horse gram)
- *Mattar/Aloo paneer* (cheese prepared with peas or potato)
- *Ambal* (a sour dish made from pumpkin, jaggery and tamarind)
- Rice and *chapati* (bread)
- Variety of pickles (mango pickle, lemon pickle, mixed pickle, *kadam* pickle etc.)
- **Delicacies:**
  - *Maa ka Madra* (yogurt-based gravy for black lentils)
  - *Mittha Madra* (made with milk, dry fruit, and semolina with sweet taste)
  - *Auryia* (a curd dish fermented by mustard seeds)
  - *Khamire* (Fermented flour bread and fried)
  - *Babroos* (prepared from flour and fried in oil with sweet taste)

Cuisines for Specific Occasions: Special Delicacies

- ***Saanti da Pat***: On the day of the marriage, during the event *Saant*, the preparation for lunch will invariably have the same items in all the houses. These are:
  - *Rajmash*
  - *Chane ki dal* (grams)
  - *Ambal* or *Maani* (a tangy preparation of mango or tamarind)
  - Curd with sprinkling of some vegetable or fried items to make it crunchy
  - *Peele Chol* (sweet yellow rice)

- **For auspicious occasions:**
  - *Keyur*: It is prepared by frying flour or refined white flour batter. It is served with sugar and curd. Even the bridegroom is welcomed by his in-laws with this as his first meal.
  - *Pugga* on *Pugge ka Vrat*
  - *Fenia*, coconut on *Karva Chauth*
  - *Revadian, gajjak* and *Til ke laddoo* (Sweet candies made of jaggery and sesame seeds) during winter festvals.

- **Delicious snacks**
  - *Kaladi*: It is milk preserved by the coagulation of proteins, then fried in a pan. It is a different form of cheese.
  - *Chille*: These are fried flour bread, sweet or saltish, and eaten during the rainy and winter seasons.
  - *Guchhiyan ka Pulao*: Fried rice with sprinkling of a special type of mushroom

- **During Winters**
  - *Makki ki roti* (maize bread)
  - *Sarson ka saag* (mustard vegetable) with lots of *ghee* (butter)
  - *Kasrod ka saag* (a special wild, hairy vegetable grown in cold hilly areas)
  - Non-Vegetarian specialty, *Khatta* meat: It is mutton cooked with sour pomegranate seeds (*anardana*) or lime juice and flavored with fumes of a burning charcoal soaked in mustard oil.

- **Sweet dishes**
    - *Pile Chol:* Sweet yellow rice
    - *Kheer:* It is a dish prepared from milk by adding rice and dry fruit. Saffron is extensively used to flavor the sweet dish and for its antioxidant benefits.
    - *Gajjar or Dal ka Halwa:* Vegetable carrot or lentils are cooked in milk till it becomes thick after evaporation of complete water.

GI (Geographical Indication) Tagged Items of Dogra Land

Genuine quality products of an area are given a GI Tag label by the Ministry of Commerce and Industry based on an international Act in line with the World Trade Organization. The purpose of GI Tag is to protect the authenticity of a product and prevent its imitation. A few of the GI Tagged products from the Dogra land are as below:

- **Basohli Paintings** are known for their unique qualities.
- **Basohli Pashmina**: These are shawls, mufflers, blankets and baskets made of Pashmina and known for their feather-like softness, light weight, durability and insulating properties.
- **Ramban Anardana**: Locally called *Dhruni,* is a wild fruit growing on hilly areas of Jammu and Kashmir and has a unique peculiar sour taste.
- **Kalari from Udhampur**: It is a very dense cheese, sauted in its own fat. It is the most relished street food snack among ethnic Dogras.
- Bhaderwah Rajma
- Rajouri Chikri Woodcraft
- Basmati rice: Famous for its sleek grains and pleasant aroma

Fig 11.2: Bridegroom riding a mare and going to the bride's house
(Source: Photo from newspaper)

Daily Food Items

Kalari

Pugga

Keyur

Fig 11.3: Typical Dogra food items
(Source: Local magazines)

Dogra Dance

Jangams: Descendents of the ones who witnessed *Shiv Vivah,*
and now recite the same on various occasions

Fig 11.4: Dogra dance and dress of *Jangams*
(*Source: Photos from local newspapers*)

Fig. 11.5: Kite Festival and Bonfire during *Lohri* function
(Source: Dept of Culture, J&K Govt.)

Mubarik Mandi, Jammu

Pink Hall of Dogra Art Museum, Jammu
Fig: 11.6: Heritage places of Jammu
(Source: Dept. of Culture, J&K Govt.)

LINGUISTIC LANDSCAPE IN J&K STATE AND DECLINE OF DOGRI LANGUAGE

J&K is a panorama of plurality, with longstanding heterogenous traditions and cultures that have been united in their diversity, its inhabitants had developed a strong sense of peaceful coexistence between its numerous religions, peoples and customs.

– EFSAS

Regional Diversity in J&K State

Till 5th August 2019, the State of Jammu and Kashmir included the region of Ladakh in its territory. However, after that, Jammu & Kashmir and Ladakh became two independent union territories (UT) of India. Hence the details covered in this chapter are for the Union Territory of J&K.

The only authentic document giving population and languages spoken in the State of Jammu and Kashmir is the Census of 1941 conducted during British rule. At that time, the State of Jammu and Kashmir comprised of the following regions:

- Jammu Region of UT of J&K
- Kashmir Region of UT of J&K
- Ladakh UT
- Pakistan occupied Jammu and Kashmir

Linguistic Diversity in Erstwhile J&K

The State of Jammu and Kashmir is geographically very diverse. It has plain areas of Jammu region, hilly areas around Jammu and the huge mountains of Pir Panchal which are extensions of Himalayas. People in different regions follow different customs and traditions. As the saying goes, that language changes after every 20 km, it can be seen here in J&K too.

Besides regions, the people staying in these areas also follow different religions with different customs and traditions. Prominent among these are Muslims, Hindus, Sikhs, Buddhists, Jains, Christians etc. All of them are living together harmoniously. They speak different languages, leading to vast linguistic diversity in the state.

Before 1947, the main regional areas in J&K were:

- Jammu
- Kashmir
- Ladakh
- Baltistan
- Gilgit

And, of course, the languages spoken in each of these regions are different. Kashmiri language was spoken in Kashmir, Dogri in Jammu region, Balti in Baltistan, Shina in Gilgit, and Ladakhi in Ladakh. Besides these, dialects were spoken in many areas of the state as under:

- Poonchi/Pahari/Potohari in Rajouri-Poonch belt
- Gojri by Gujjars, spread over the hilly areas
- Bhaderwahi, Bhalesi and Curahi
- Padari in Padar region of Kishtwar. It has similarity with the dialect Pangwali spoken in Pangi Valley in Chamba (H.P)
- Siraji dialect spoken in north of river Chenab between Ramban and Bhart on the way to Kishtwar
- Rambani, as the name suggests, is the dialect spoken around Ramban and has largely Punjabi pronunciation.

- Poguli is a language spoken in a small area to the East of Ramsu. It resembles Kashmiri though the accent is a little different from the Kashmiri language.
- Shina in the Gurez Valley, a couple of villages in Tral and the Sarbal village in Sonamarg. There is also a small community of Shina people who live in Srinagar city. However, Shina is the main language of people in Gilgit which is now in Pakistan.

Languages of J&K in 1941

Details of the languages spoken in J&K during the 19th and early 20th centuries are not very clear, However, the Census of J&K in 1941 gives a fair idea of the languages and the number of people speaking those languages. The population of Jammu & Kashmir (including Ladakh UT, and POJK) was 40,21,616 and the languages spoken by them, as interpreted by the linguistic analysts, are tabulated Table 12.1.

Table 12.1: Major Linguistic Population of J&K in 1941

S.No.	Language	Kashmir Province	Jammu Province	Ladakh & Baltistan	Gilgit Region	Total
1.	Kashmiri	13,69,537	1,17,380	1,173	323	15,49,460
2.	Dogri	73,473	10,00,018	453	1,329	10,75,273
3.	Western Pahari (Variant of Dogri and Punjabi)	1,70,432	3,60,870	5	12	5,31,319
4.	Hindustani (Hindi and Urdu)	10,631	1,67,368	22	507	1,78,529
5.	Rajasthani (Gujari)	92,392	1,87,890	0	3,369	2,83,741
6.	Balti	352	184	5	5	82,993
7.	Shina (Dardic)	7,888	14	13,562	63,040	84,604
8.	Lahnda (Pothwari)	8	82,975	5	5	82,993
9.	Ladakhi	230	229	46,420	4	46,953
10.	Burushaski	3	0	244	32,885	33,132
11.	Tibetan	6	145	317	15	503

Languages of J&K After 1947

After 1947, one third of J&K was annexed by Pakistan, so the language diversity got changed after that. Kashmiri and Dogri and their dialects remained the main languages of the region and in the Census of 1951, the linguistic experts interpolated that Kashmiri was spoken by 24,95,487 persons whereas Dogri was spoken by 13,00,000 persons.

However, the new govt. which took over the reigns of J&K after 1947 was anti Dogras, so it did not allow Dogri language to flourish. The govt. got Kashmiri and Urdu languages included in the 8th Schedule of the Indian Constitution, giving the national status to both these languages and Dogri was left behind. It was not made even the State language of J&K.

So, census after census, which is conducted every 10 years, the pace of Kashmiri speaking people in the state kept on increasing and Dogri could not match that pace.

The people of Jammu kept on struggling to get proper place for the Dogri language which was deprived in 1947. In 2003, when the Govt of Atal Bihari Vajpayee came in the Centre, Dogri language got its place and was included in the 8th Schedule of The Indian Constitution. As it gained national importance, it was thought that the State govt. would make this language compulsory in all the schools, but that did not happen. There was no thrust from the govt. side. Some people were seen saying that the inclusion in the 8th Schedule was only on paper with zero effect on the ground.

However, despite that, the main languages in the erstwhile State of Jammu & Kashmir remained as Kashmiri and Dogri and their variants. Other languages were spoken by a smaller population in the state.

Despite these difficulties, Dogri language continued to maintain its presence to some extent. According to the most recent Census of 2011, the combined population of the Union Territories of Jammu & Kashmir and Ladakh was 1,25,41,302 and the languages spoken by this population are listed in Table 12.2.

It could be seen that between the Census of 1951 and 2011, the Kashmiri speaking population increased by 2.65 times whereas Dogri speaking persons increased by only 1.93 times only. Between 1951 and 1961, the Dogri speaking population had even shown negative growth, details of which are covered in the next chapter.

Table 12.2: Languages spoken in J&K as per Census of 2011

S.No	Language	Number of Speakers	Percent of Speakers
1.	Kashmiri	66,080,837	53.27
2.	Dogri	25,13,712	20.04
3.	Hindi	26,12,631	20.83
4.	Punjabi	2,19,193	1.75
5.	Urdu	19,956	0.16

Balance less than 4% spoke other national languages in J&K

Decline of Dogri

A study has been carried out to figure out all the reasons for the Dogri language speakers showing a negative growth during 1951-1961 and comparatively less growth as compared to other languages viz. Kashmiri subsequently. A few of these are explained below.

a. **Anti-Dogra Attitude of Govt.:** During the reign of Maharaja Hari Singh from 1925 to 1947, anti-Maharaja groups were brewing up in the State. Sheikh Mohd. Abdullah, the President of All J&K Muslim Conference agitated against the Dogra ruler several times and wanted self-rule for Kashmir. In 1946, he launched the "Quit Kashmir Movement" against Maharaja.

   On 26 Oct 1947, J&K signed the instrument of accession and became part of India. Maharaja Hari Singh willingly went into exile and Sheikh Mohd. Abdullah, later was elected as the first Prime Minister of J&K. As per Dr. Karan Singh, the then Sadr-e-Riyasat of J&K, Sheikh Abdullah was anti-Dogras and used to abuse them on many occasions. During his tenure as head of the state, he pushed

Dogri to a lower level and made Urdu and English as the official languages of J&K.

b. **Domination by Larger Area:** Dogra region of Jammu was part of Jammu & Kashmir State. Kashmir province (including Ladakh) was bigger in area and population and hence always dominated Duggar land. Since 1947, the Prime Minister/Chief Minister of J&K State had always been from Kashmir (except for two and a half years during 2005 to 2008 when Ghulam Nabi Azad was the Chief Minister) who gave preference to Kashmiri sidelining the Dogri language. This language never got any official recognition for at least 55 years after independence.

Number of Ministers speaking Kashmiri language in the govt. of J&K were always more than the Dogri speaking Ministers. So, Dogri language was not a priority for them which slowly and steadily started losing its hold on ground.

c. **Declined National Status:** At the time of bifurcation of India in two countries in 1947, over 563 princely states opted to join Indian Union with J&K being the biggest of all these. Its official languages were Dogri and Urdu and the State had a Dogra king as its ruler. However, when Sheikh Mohd. Abdullah became the Prime Minister of the State; he demoted the language and never allowed it to become a national or state language. He got Kashmiri language included in the 8th Schedule of the Constitution of India and made Urdu and English as the official languages of the State.

Dogri, thus lost its status at the national as well as the state levels. It was reduced to an optional subject in schools and was never made a compulsory subject. Thus, the new generations of Dogras got debarred from studying this language at the school/college level leading to the shrinking of the Dogra population.

d. **International Influence:** Pakistan had always been laying its claim over the state of Jammu and Kashmir on the presumption that most of the Kashmiri people want to join Pakistan. This led the Indian govt. to pump in a lot of money in the state. It always proved to the world that Kashmiri people like to stay with India and not Pakistan. Most of the funds which came to the state from the central govt. were thus diverted to Kashmir region and not Jammu, primarily to win the popularity of Kashmiris.

This fact also kept the Jammu region out of the limelight. Jobs for the Dogri speaking people got reduced drastically with the result that students started preferring other languages than Dogri.

e. **Debarring Right of Children to Education**: Under "Right of Children to Free Education Act 2009", all the students in govt. schools (and 25% students in private schools), are given education free up to class 8th (Right of Free Education Act, 2009). They are given uniforms as well as books free of cost. However, as far as Dogri language is concerned, books are provided free only up to class 2, thus giving no incentive to students who want to study Dogri, despite it being an official language of J&K UT with national status as a scheduled language.

Besides this, there is no check on the private schools who blatantly defy the orders contained in the above Act. To attract more children, they prefer to teach French, German and other foreign languages than Dogri. This also results in degradation of Dogri.

f. **Promoting Arabic and Persian Languages in the State:** As per the Census Report of 2011, there is no citizen of J&K whose mother tongue is Persian (an Iranian language). Still the Education Dept. of J&K has been creating posts for this language for the schools of Jammu and Kashmir.

Even the Arabic speaking population in the State is less than 200 and that too they are the senior citizens. Still the govt. of J&K has continuously been creating posts for them in the schools. Even during 2024, advertisement was floated by the govt. for six posts in Arabic and Persian Languages in schools.

During December 2024, an order was issued by the govt. to introduce Arabic subjects in Govt. Hari Singh Higher Secondary School, Residency Road, Jammu, which is in the heart of the city of Jammu.

Thus, the attitude of the govt. to promote Arabic and Persian subjects in schools at the cost of Dogri subject has demoted the language further to the back seat among children.

g. **Administrators Forced to Learn Urdu & Not Dogri:** Govt. Administrators, JKAS (erstwhile KAS) qualified officers who run the administration of the State of Jammu and Kashmir were forced to learn Urdu language and not Dogri. Even the IAS (Indian Administration Service), most of whom are not from J&K State were also forced to learn Urdu to run the administration in the state. This trend at the officers' level also discouraged the Dogras to learn Dogri language in schools and colleges.

h. **Land Records not in Dogri**: During Mughal times, Jammu was under their rule for some time. So, the Persian language got its roots in Jammu. Later Urdu replaced Persian, and all the land records were prepared in Urdu language. These records are Sale/Purchase deed, *Jamabandi, Intekaal, Gardawri* etc. and were not translated in Dogri or any other language till 2020.

It became mandatory for all revenue dept. officials to know Urdu. Knowledge of Urdu was mandatory for the posts of *Patwari, Girdawar* or the *Naib Tehsildar.* Graduate students in Jammu were attracted to learn Urdu at the cost of their own language Dogri so that they could get employment in the Revenue Dept. These posts are very lucrative too.

This fact also moved students away from the Dogri language.

i. **Lack of jobs for Dogri Language:** There are over 18,000 schools in J&K. Each school should have at least one Dogri subject teacher, this being the official language of J&K. But the number of Dogri teachers is restricted to just a few hundred.

Besides this, Dogri being an official language of the state, all the govt. orders, court orders, govt. notices etc. should be translated into Dogri for dissemination to the public. Even the public announcement and advertisements on the radio and television should be in Dogri, but on grounds it is not being done.

The lackadaisical attitude of the govt. towards the Dogri language has resulted in shrinking jobs for Dogri-learning students. Students are thus forced to learn other languages to seek jobs.

j. **Migration of Dogra community to other areas:** Due to scarcity of jobs for Dogri-trained citizens, they are forced to learn English/ Hindi languages which have more jobs outside the state. So. migration of Dogra students to other states becomes natural, resulting in a change in demography of the region besides reduction of Dogra population in the state.

k. **No Dogri TV Satellite Channel:** For the entertainment and education of the locals and promotion of regional culture, Door Darshan has 35 TV satellite channels. Besides news readers, there are other local artists, singers, professionals etc. who produce programmes in local languages for transmission in such a way that locals staying in the far-flung areas can also remain connected to their culture. This also provides employment for local artists.

Out of 35 satellite channels, 7 are dedicated for national and international programmes whereas balance 28 are for covering cultures enshrined in 22 main languages of 8th Schedule of Indian Constitution. It is surprising to see that there is no dedicated TV satellite channel even though Dogri is one of the 22 scheduled languages.

l. **Negative Narrative:** After 1947, a negative narrative was created for the Dogri language. It was very common to hear sentences like Dogras are *anpad* (illiterate), *graayeen* (villagers) or *dungers* (animals). Even the Dogras fell prey to this narrative and started associating themselves with other so-called superior and dominating languages like English and Hindi. This resulted in even the Dogras asking their children to study English and Hindi languages in schools and not the Dogri language.

Death of Dogri Script viz. Takri

The original script of Dogri language is *Takri*. This script originated from Sharda script and related to *Gurmukhi* script (in which Punjabi language is written) and *Lahnda* script. Its emergence is recorded in the 16th century and since then has been used to write Dogri language. It was also used to write other Pahari languages like Jaunsari, Kulvi, Chambeali etc. It was an official script in parts of North and Northwestern Indian States from the 17th century till the mid-20th century. As per a study report, there were 13 different versions of Takri, however, the Takri used for Dogri was very popular.

A version of Takri, called Chambeali, was the official script of erstwhile Chamba State. Till 1930, it was taught in the State High School, Chamba in primary classes and a permanent teacher was employed to teach Takri. During this time, various primers and multiplication tables were edited in Takri and printed by Sh. Bakshi Ram Malhotra. Even in the revenue dept. an official *patwari* was employed till 2006 who could translate land documents written in Takri.

The Takri version of Jammu region was named as *Namme Dogra Akkhar*. Its numerals and alphabets are shown in Fig 12.1.

Dr. J. Voghel has described a stone inscription in Takri script at "Salhi on Sechu Nallah" dated 1160 CE as evidence of use of Takri even in ancient times. Even Amir Khusro's Masnavi Nuh-Sipihir (1253-1325) talks of Dogri as one of the important languages of this region.

During the 16th and 19th centuries, Takri was also used in some parts of Punjab and Himachal Pradesh. It was used for keeping business records (*Bahi Khatas*), writing administrative documents like letters, copper-plate land grants and official decrees. It was used on postage stamps that can still be seen on many inscriptions on temples of Jammu and Basohli paintings.

Maharaja Ranbir Singh, during his reign of Jammu and Kashmir, found some inconsistencies in Takri. There were no *matras* and vowel combinations were absent. With the help of Shri Vishweshwar Jyotsi, Principal, Ranbir Pathshala Jammu, he standardized it and reformed it to be used and read by all. Many documents were translated into Takri script for the benefit of the locals. He also started teaching this script in Raghunath Pathshala and employees were encouraged to learn this language.

Vidya Vilas Press, established by Maharaja Pratap Singh, has many books translated in Takri. Some of the important books translated are *Leelavati* a treatise on mathematics, *Ranbir Chikitsa*, *Vyavhar Gita, Qanoon Zabta Dewan, Niyam Sena Vibhag, Ranbir Dand Vidhi. Praveshika* etc. A Dogri newspaper *Dogra Mittra* was published in 1889. In the 20th century, a missionary of Scotland published a book *Mangal Samachar* in Takri script.

Maharaja Ranbir Singh himself used to sign in Takri. Petitions read out in Maharaja's court were replaced from Persian to *Namme Dogra Akkhar.*

After his death, Maharaj Pratap Singh and Maharaja Hari Singh could not take this script to the public. But under pressure of British government, Urdu language was given more weightage and made as the official language. In earlier years even the Persian language was introduced in J&K. It was seen as an after effect of Mughal rule in J&K during earlier centuries.

As per some documents, Takri script was replaced by *Devnagri* script in Jammu in 1944. In the State of Himachal Pradesh, Takri script was also used for Dogri as well as other dialects of Dogri. They also replaced it with *Devnagri* script in 1948.

Since then, Takri is on the death bed, revival efforts for which are going on in some pockets of Jammu and Himachal Pradesh.

Current Status of Dogri Language

On paper, Dogri has got the national status since 2003 when it was included in the 8th Schedule of the Constitution of India. It was also declared as one of the five official languages of the UT of Jammu and Kashmir in 2020. Civil society forced the government to take certain concrete steps on ground so that the Dogri language retains its glory.

However, on certain occasions, the reversal of the language is also seen. As per a news report from 2024, a linguistic survey conducted in Jammu city revealed that only 10% of the population speaks the Dogri language, while 90% communicate in other languages such as Hindi and Punjabi. Among the 10% Dogri speakers, only 1% are below 60 years of age, with the majority being senior citizens over the age of 60.

Civil society has already started finding the reasons for the same. In a physical survey of schools in Jammu city, conducted by them revealed that even though Dogri books are supplied in govt. schools up to class 2nd, hardly any student knows or speaks Dogri fluently. Even the teachers shy away from speaking in Dogri language. As regards private schools, they prefer to teach French or German language to the students to impress parents and attract more students but would not teach Dogri.

The second reason they found is the non-implementation of the National Education Policy-2020 by the schools. As per this policy, the native language must be taught up to Class 5 and preferably up to Class 8, which they are not following in the absence of any direction from the state government. Govt. has been approached to issued policy decision.

International Coding of Takri Script

At the global level, alphabets of all the languages of the world are given unique codes by an organization named Unicode Consortium. The aim of this codification is to standardize the alphabets so that they follow some standard called Unicode Standard. Till date, 168 languages/scripts with 1,54,998 characters have been given Unicode Number. These scripts are given a unique name called Block. So, the latest version 16.0 defines 338 blocks including 164 in the Basic Multilingual Plane (BMP), 161 in the Supplementary Multilingual Plane (SMP), and 7 in the Supplementary Ideographic Plane (SIP).

Preliminary proposal to encode the Takri script (for Dogri language) in Unicode was submitted by Anshuman Pandey, University of California, Berkeley, California, USA on 30 July 2015. He submitted another proposal on 04 Nov 2015. Later, on 25 June 2017, Srinidhi and Sridatta submitted another proposal for encoding Takri.

After due deliberations by the authorities and the receipt of additional details, Takri script was added to Unicode in June 2018 when its 11.0 version was released. The name of the Block given to Takri script was DOGRA Block. Each alphabet of Takri script is given a unique Unicode number. These numbers are referred to as U+11800 to U+1184F (Hexadecimal number) and contain 60 characters.

Code numbers for alphabets of Takri script, character wise are:
U+11800, U+11801, U+11802,....,U=11809, U+1180A, U+1180B,. ., U+1180F
U+11810, U+11811, U+11813,..., U+11819, U+1181A, U+1181B,.., U+1181F

And so on.
Details of actions taken to revive Takri script are covered in the next chapter.

Fig 12.1: Alphabets of Takri script
(Source: Wikipedia website)

Fig. 12.2: Unicode numbers of alphabets of Takri under DOGRA Block
(Source: Wikipedia website)

Chapter 13

REVIVAL OF DOGRI: INITIATIVES OF GOVT. AND NGOS

"Culture makes people understand each other better.
And if they understand each other better in their soul,
it is easier to overcome the economic and political barriers."

– Paulo Coelho

After 1947, Dogri lost its official status as it was neither retained as the official language of the State of J&K, nor any national status given to it. However, the schools were given the liberty to teach it in case they wanted to do so. In the bargain, private schools almost stopped teaching of Dogri and stressed more on English, Hindi and Urdu languages as these had national importance being included in the 8th Schedule of the Indian Constitution.

Many NGOs had visualized the debacle which Dogri language would face. So, they started taking preemptive actions so that the language does not become extinct, and the Dogra culture remains vibrant. One of the prominent NGOs, established during 1944 was Dogri Sanstha which spearheaded the revival movement.

Origin of Dogri Sanstha

To create awareness about the rich cultural heritage of Dogras, some enthusiastic Dogras got collected and established an organization named Dogri Sanstha on 29th Jan 1944. Initially, it did not have suitable accommodation for the office, so it operated from personal residences or hired buildings. In 1971, Dr. Karan Singh came to the rescue of Sanstha, donated land at Karan Nagar, Jammu where Dogri Bhawan was constructed and its operations commenced from there in 1982.

During the partition of the country in 1947, it played a great role in arousing the sentiments of the people by holding *Kavi Sammellans* and staging dramas in different parts of Jammu. It also promoted Pahari paintings and was instrumental in the setting up of the Dogra Art Gallery, presently in Jammu. Its main activities and outcomes have been as under:

- It laid stress on the publication of Dogri literature. Its first publication, "Jaago Duggar" came up during that time and till date it has published close to 200 books.
- It brings out the Dogri magazine *Nameen Chetana* and to date over 200 volumes have been published.
- It has been organizing All India Dogri Writers Conferences, symposia, seminars, debates and declamation contests.
- It also organizes literary meets and *Gazal Goshtis.*
- It provides free books and guidance to students.
- It conducts free coaching classes for the Shiromani classes
- It fought for getting the Dogri language included in the 8th Schedule of the Indian Constitution and got success in 2003 when the Govt. of India acceded to the request and included it in the 8th Schedule of the Indian Constitution, thus giving it a national status.
- During 2024, it also conducted an internship program for undergraduate students pursuing Dogri courses.

Presently Padma Shri Prof. Lalit Magotra is the President of the Sanstha and Mr. Rajeshwar is the General Secretary.

Bringing Dogri in Education System

Reference of Dogri is seen on the copper plates of the 11th century, unearthed in Chamba adjoining the Jammu region. In the linguistic survey of Amir Khusro in 1317, the language spoken by the Dogras had been referred as "Duggar Bhasha"

However, in the formal education system, the impetus was given during the reign of Maharaja Ranbir Singh (1856-1885), when he introduced Dogri language as a subject to be taught in the Ranbir Pathshala. All the govt. officials were asked to take on the studies of Dogri, script for which was a modified version of Takri called *Namme Dogra Akkhar.* Later, it was introduced as a subject in schools.

After 1947, though it remained in schools as a subject, its status continued going down when it was changed from a compulsory subject to an optional subject. Private schools which attract bulk of the students in big cities and towns stopped teaching Dogri as a compulsory subject. In most of the schools in Jammu city, it is not taught also.

To give push to the knowledge of Dogri, Dogri Sanstha convinced the govt. to start an examination of *Tilak*, which was considered as 'Proficiency in Dogri'. It was started by the University of Jammu & Kashmir in 1964. Within a gap of two years, two more examinations named *Preveen* and *Shiromani* which were equivalent to 'High Proficiency' and 'Honors' respectively were started by the University.

Syllabi and books for these exams were prepared by Prof. Ram Nath Shastri on behalf of Dogri Sanstha. Even free coaching classes were conducted by the Sanstha right from 1964 onwards.

Introducing Dogri at University Level

In 1969, the Govt. of J&K came up with *J&K Universities Act 1969* under which University of Jammu and Kashmir was bifurcated into two universities viz. University of Kashmir and University of Jammu. The University of Jammu was located in the heart of the Dogra land i.e.

Jammu city. With this university coming to Jammu region, more and more students of Jammu province got the opportunity of getting higher education near to their home. Presently, it has its off campuses in various district headquarters of Jammu province.

It started offering programmes from Diploma to Ph.D levels on various subjects. To promote Dogri language, and Dogra culture, a Dogri Research Cell was established in the University of Jammu in 1971. It started conducting research on Dogra culture. Year wise progress made since then is given below.

- 1971: Dogri Research Cell was established and one post of Senior Fellow in Dogri was sanctioned. Prof. Ram Nath Shastri was appointed as Senior Fellow in Research.
- 1975: The Dogri Research Cell was upgraded to the Dogri Research Centre. Director Bal Krishan Shastry joined as Director-cum-Senior Fellow in Dogri.
- 1976: Dr. Veena Gupta also joined the Research Centre as Fellow in Dogri
- 1980: Dr. Champa Sharma joined as Director-cum-Senior Fellow in Dogri after the retirement of Dr. Bal Krishan Shastry.
- 1983: Dogri Research Centre was upgraded to a Post-Graduate Dept. of Dogri.

This department, since then, has been teaching students, conducting research on a variety of aspects like language, literature, culture, history, folklore, conducting research workshops and organizing national and international seminars.

To start with, in the 1980s, it published a book titled *Hindi-Dogri Conversational Guide*. In a couple of years it published 7 books in Dogri, two volumes of Dogri Research Journals *Dogri Shod* and started producing Ph.D qualified scholars. Very recently, it translated the Constitution of India in Dogri also.

Recognition of Language and Institution of Awards

As the language had no official status, Dogri Sanstha strived hard to get it recognized at various levels. Outcomes are as under:

- **Recognition by Sahitya Academi**: In 1969, Dogri language was recognized by Sahitya Academi, New Delhi as an independent literary language. Since then, writers have been encouraged to produce good language books so that they could get awards. Sh. Narendra Khajuria was the first Dogri writer to be awarded in 1970 for his short stories titled *Nile Amhar Kale Badal.*

  Till date already 23 writers have got Sahitya Academy Awards in Dogri. Sahitya Academi has now introduced awards in many categories. Names of a few of the categories and the recipients for the year 2024 are as under:
  - The Sahitya Academy Fellowship - Sh. Ved Rahi, Dogri writer- and poet
  - Sahitya Academi Translation Award - Ms. Sushma Rani
  - Sahitya Academi Bal Sahitya Puruskar - Sh. Bishan Singh "Dardi"
  - Sahitya Academi Yuva Puruskar - Ms. Heena Choudhary

- **J&K Govt. Awards**: The Govt. of J&K also announced its awards on 26th January 2024. Its Dogra recipients are as under:
  - Lifetime Achievement Award - Padma Shri S.P.Verma
  - Award for Dogri writing - Sh. Inderjit Kesar and Sh. Mohan Singh

- **Dogri Sanstha**: It has also instituted many awards for encouraging writers, poets, artists, painters, media personnel etc. who promote Dogri culture.

- **Included in the Constitution of India**: In 2003, It was included in the 8th Schedule of the Constitution of India, thus upgrading to national level at par with other 21 scheduled languages of the country

- **Declared Official Language in J&K**: In 2020, Lt. Governor, J&K made Dogri language as the official language of J&K in addition to other four languages which are English, Hindi, Urdu and Kashmiri.

With this, Dogra writers got the incentive to write more books in Dogri language and the students/aspirants got the opportunity to appear in competitive examinations like IAS and JKAS.

Besides above, it has been seen that eminent Dogra personalities are also recognized at the national level and awarded the Padma Shri award for their work in promotion of Dogra culture. A few of the awardees of Padma Shri are as under:

- 2025: Prof. Lalit Magotra, President Dogri Sanstha for his contribution towards Dogri language.
- 2024: Mr. Romalo Ram, a Dogri Folk Artist from Jammu for reviving the dying folk Form "Geetru and Bhakh"
- 2023: Mr. Mohan Singh Salathia for his work in promoting drama, theatre, and literature
- 2020: Mr. Shiv Datt Nirmohi, a Dogra writer for his works in Dogri art, culture, and history of Jammu
- Other Dogras who were awarded the Padma Shri award included Smt. Padma Sachdev, Prof. Ved Kumari Ghai, Prof. Vishwamurti Shastri, Sh. Balwant Thakur, Prof. Ram Nath Shastri, Sh. Nilamber Dev Sharma besides others.

In February 2025, Sh. Om Birla, Speaker of the Lok Sabha announced that from now onwards the online translation of Lok Sabha Proceedings in Dogri and other 21 Scheduled Languages will be available to all the members. This act will also promote Dogri at national level. Even the monthly address of Sh. Narendra Modi, Prime Minister of India, to the nation will be translated in Dogri language from 23rd February 2025 onwards.

Placement for Dogri knowing Persons

With the commencement of teaching of Dogri in colleges and University, many job opportunities for the Dogri educated students opened. Main areas for their placement are in the following fields:

- Schools, colleges and universities as teaching faculty
- Radio, television, and other multimedia agencies
- With the introduction of Dogri as a subject in prestigious examinations like IAS and JKAS, aspirants started joining state as well as national administrations through these examinations.
- As a writer, actor, director etc. in Dogri dramas and films
- In the Parliament of India for online translation of speeches to Dogri
- For translation of Prime Minister's monthly address to the nation "Man ki Baat"
- At CIIL, Mysore, for preparing Dogri academic books. Already one book called *Dogri Kayida* was published by them in December 2024. Many more academic books are yet to be published.

J&K Academy of Art, Culture and Languages

In the absence of any Director of Culture or Dept of Culture in the Government, J&K Academy of Art, Culture and Languages was formed in 1958. The aim of the academy was to promote the regional culture and languages of each region of J&K. In 1963, it was declared as an autonomous corporate body. To give maximum freedom to the Academy so that it works as an independent body, it was converted to a society and registered under the Societies Registration Act.

This academy supports all the regional languages spoken in J&K, Dogri being one of them. Its main office is in Jammu city and the sub offices are located at Srinagar, Rajouri, Kathua, and Doda. It involves itself in the promotion of the culture of each region of the state with special reference to:

- Language and literature
- Music, dance and other performing arts including theatre
- Visual, creative and fine arts

Dogra Art Museum

Dogra Art Museum, previously known as Art Gallery, was inaugurated in 1964 by Dr. Rajendra Prasad, President of India. It houses the vintage items of Dogra culture which are:

- Miniature paintings from Basohli
- Manuscripts
- Coins
- Jewelry
- Portrait of Jammu rulers
- Terracotta heads from Akhnoor
- Arms and armory

Over 7,000 items depicting Dogra culture of ancient times are kept here. Presently, this museum is located at Mubarak Mandi, Jammu

Department of Culture

To give a boost to the local culture, the Govt. of J&K established a full-fledged Dept. of Culture in 2008. The primary mandate given to the dept. is to preserve, develop and promote the tangible and intangible art and cultural heritage of Jammu and Kashmir. To perform its role, it has set the following tasks for it:

- Maintenance and conservation of heritage, historic sites, ancient monuments, manuscripts, and artefacts
- Administration of libraries
- Promotion of literary, visual and performing arts

Promotion of institutional and individual non-official initiatives in art and culture. The functional spectrum of the Department envisages creating cultural awareness from the grass root level. The following Directorates/Academy work under it:

- Directorate of Archives, Archaeology and Museums
- Directorate of Libraries and Research
- J&K Academy of Art, Culture, and Languages

Ancient Monuments Preservation Act 1920

The government also encourages the younger generation to serve as ambassadors of J&K's cultural legacy. The goal is to highlight the value of cultural heritage and encourage respect and understanding amongst communities. It has launched the following schemes:

- Scheme of Financial Assistance for the Preservation of Old Manuscripts, Literature, Art & Crafts. It provides financial assistance to preserve old manuscripts, literature, art, and crafts.
- Financial Assistance for Preservation and Development of Cultural Heritage of the Himalayas. It provides financial assistance to preserve and develop cultural heritage.
- Heritage Conservation and Preservation Act, 2010. This act aims to preserve the state's tangible and intangible heritage, such as buildings, monuments, artifacts, and traditional knowledge systems. It also classifies heritage based on its significance and determines how to preserve it.

Some of the Dogra heritage sites are shown on Fig. 13.1.

Tribal Affairs Dept. J&K

Many Dogri speaking tribes have no access to modern facilities. Considering this, the govt. of J&K has established a full-fledged dept. of Tribal Affairs to address the needs of all the tribal groups and their languages.

Its vision is to develop a society which offers a conducive and stimulating atmosphere for growth and development, in a safe and protective environment, ensuring dignified life to the Scheduled Tribe population. This is achieved by promoting social and economic empowerment of all the tribes through various policies.

It aims to provide social security and institutional support to them including an equitable environment for development, growth and education. Financial support to school going children is also provided besides marketing support to the local products through State Tribal Development Cooperative Corporations.

It has special schemes for providing social security to the elderly people, residential facilities for the students in the form of hostels and imparting vocational training to them.

Prominent Local Organizations Promoting Dogra Culture

Besides the initiatives of the govt. and the organizations mentioned above, there are many other organizations which are involved in preserving the Dogra culture and showcasing it to the entire world. Works of a few of these organizations have been given here.

Shri Mata Vaishno Devi Shrine Board (SMVDSB)

The shrine of Shri Mata Vaishno Devi in the Trikuta hills at Katra, J&K is a great heritage temple for Dogras, which now is revered by all in the country. To administer its functioning and facilitate the pilgrims, SMVD Shrine Board was formed in 1986. Its popularity has spread so much all over the world that the number of pilgrims visiting it has gone over 10 million each year. It provides the following facilities to all including the Dogras of the region:

- Provides employment to thousand to locals
- Opened a university for providing higher education for all
- Opened a superspeciality hospital for the healthcare of the locals
- Runs a nursing college for girls, a Gurukul for boys and provides help to many women self-help groups
- Provides help to schools and temples in Dogra region
- Took responsibility of around 150 girl children who were born during 2011, the Silver Jubilee Year of the formation of SMVDSB. It made a fixed deposit of Rs. 1,00,000 in the name of each of the children. Besides this, it gives Rs. 500 per month to each parent

so that they take care of and provide education to the girl child. This facility will be available to them till they reach the age of 18 years.

- At the time of the marriage of the daughters of *Baridars,* the erstwhile caretakers of the shrine, the Board provides financial assistance to each one of them.

J&K Dharmarth Trust

This trust was started by Maharaja Gulab Singh of J&K in 1846. It has built temples, mostly in the Jammu region. Presently it looks after 125 temples which are the heritage temples of Dogras. It helps the locals by way of:

- providing employment to around 500 locals
- providing space to locals for performing religious rituals
- keeping the Dogra culture alive

Dr. Karan Singh is the main Trustee and Brig R.S Langhe is the President of the Thrust.

Dogra Sadar Sabha

It was founded in 1904 during the reign of Maharaja Pratap Singh. Its main role is to preserve the interest of the Dogra community and have camaraderie among various communities in the State of J&K. During the first 100 years of its formation, it went through many ups and downs, however, now it has become stable and pursuing its aim of serving the Dogra community and promoting their culture.

Sh. Gulchain Singh Charak, former Cabinet Minister of J&K State, is the President of the Sabha.

Other Organizations

Besides the above, many other organizations and individuals have come forward for the promotion of this culture. Some of these are:

- Dogra Brahmin Pratinidhi Sabha
- Mahajan Sabha
- Dogra Rajput Sabha
- All J&K Kashyap Rajput Sabha
- Yuva Rajput Sabha
- And many more

Organizations Active during 2023-25

The authors of this book are Dogras who have travelled all over the country and many parts of the world. However, for the past 17 years, one of the authors, Shiv Kumar, has been continuously residing in Jammu city and very active in the promotion of the Dogra culture. The organizations which he has seen closely, and are promoting Dogra culture have been explained here.

Senior Citizens SS Club, Chowadi, Jammu

This club has recently been formed by Dr. Kasturi Lal, retired Principal of Govt. Medical College, Jammu, India. A study carried out by him and his team members including one of the authors, Mr. Shiv Kumar, depicted that Dogri language was losing its ground at a very fast pace and the original script Takri is almost extinct. The younger generation is not speaking this language, and the schools are also not giving any importance to it.

To revive Dogri language, members of this club physically go to schools and conduct Dogri poem competitions, a method adopted by them to generate interest among younger generations. Besides this they promote Dogra culture by way of:

- Conducting Dogri Essay Competition in schools
- Conducting Dogri dress and Dogri *Saafa* (turban) tying completions among school students. (Fig. 13.2)
- Making display boards in Takri script and placing these at various most-visited spots in Jammu city, primarily to revive the almost extinct script.
- Interacting with many segments of the society and involving them in this drive of reviving Dogri language

Dr. Kasturi Lal is arranging ample financial resources and giving lucrative prizes to students who participate in events organized by him and also follow Dogra culture. This gesture has been appreciated by all in society. Main office bearers of this club are:

- Major General Shiv Kumar Sharma – President
- Dr. Vijay Sharma – General Secretary
- Sh. H.C. Vaid - Treasurer

Parmeshwari Care and Cure Charitable Trust:

This trust has been deeply involved in making the local public aware of the declining Dogra culture and suggesting to them the methodology to revive it. Prof. Kul Bhushan Mohtra, Managing Director of this Trust, advocates that the unique dress worn by Dogras is their identity and should be worn by all during main occasions. It keeps donating *Saafas* so that the Dogras wear it during the Dogra functions.

In December 2024, it organized a very big programme, in collaboration with The American University, USA and honored those Dogras at Jammu who were devoting their energies selflessly for the cause of Dogras.

Prof. Mohtra is also working on a project of social service, under which it plans to set up an "Elderly Studio" for the benefit of the aged people, whose children have gone out of the country for education and job purposes. These people are feeling lonely at this stage of life when support is necessary in their day-to-day activities. Accommodation planned by him will be at par with a three-star accommodation, besides a *yoga* center, a meeting hall, 24/7 dispensary, and also three time meals as per the requirement of the aged persons.

Duggar Manch

This organization, headed by Padma Shri Mohan Singh Salathia, is spearheading and promoting Dogra culture by conducting a variety of Dogri programmes. It celebrates the birth anniversaries of Dogri poets, participates in rallies voicing Dogra issues, conducts Dogri essay competitions etc. As convener of Dogri Board at Sahitya Academi, Mr. Salathia has organized many symposia and seminars for Dogri language.

Team Jammu

This team is headed by Sh. Zorawar Singh Jamwal and takes on social issues concerning Dogra youth. It conducts many awareness programs to help the Dogra youth who are prey to drug abuse. It has also collaborated with other like-minded organizations which take on the Dogra issues.

It is trying to unite the Dogra clubs outside Jammu. During February 2025, it promoted a program *Duggar Malati* at JNU Convention Centre, Delhi in collaboration with Dogra Samaj Trust and other organizations. The audience was spell bound by the performance of Dogri artists.

MIET Dogri Cultural Club (MDCC)

It is a club started by the students at Model Institute of Engineering and Technology (Autonomous), Jammu to promote Dogra culture among college students and keep it alive. During 2024, it conducted the following programmes:

- Entertainment program for 150 students singing Dogri songs, performing Dogri dance, skits in Dogri etc.

- Started an online signature campaign for making Dogri compulsory in schools of Jammu.
- Conducted Dogri essay competitions in schools.
- Covered online programs of schools celebrating Dogri Manyata Week during December 2024.
- Started going to local schools to conduct Dogri Essay Competition among children and then giving them the certificates and prizes. That way they aroused the interest of the school students in their mother tongue, Dogri.

For their promotion of the Dogra culture, The American University, USA on recommendation of The World Governing Council of Governors & Senate members of the UN University for Global Peace has awarded the certificates to nine members of MDCC.

Other Prominent Organizations

Besides, there are many other organizations like *Natrang*, Duggar Vikas Manch, Door Darshan Approved Drama Artists Association, Ram Leela Club Sainik Colony, Sarswati Dramatic Club, Billu Mandir, Dogri Bhasha Academy etc. which are promoting cause of the Dogras.

Nami Dogri Sanstha under the Presidentship of Advocate Harish Kaila is also very active in organizing Dogra cultural events.

Some of the apolitical personalities who were in the news during 2024-25 are shown in Fig 13.3.

Contribution of Shiv Kumar, Co-author of the Book

Shiv Kumar Sharma has been very actively involved in promoting Dogra values. While on active service in the Indian Army as an officer, he motivated people for selfless service to the society and organized many activities in that direction. To name a few are the blood donation drives, plantation drives, help to hearing impaired, blind children and economically backward segments of the society. He also participated in rescuing the people and the property during natural calamities like floods in Gujarat.

His services have been recognized many times, and he was honored with befitting awards by the prominent personalities and the organizations, salient of which are as under:

- Ati Vishisht Seva Medal (AVSM) by the President of India
- Commendation by the Governor of the State of Gujarat
- Commendations by the Chief of the Army Staff and GOC-in-C Army Training Command, Indian Army
- Duggar Gourav Samman Award by The American University, USA

Since his superannuation, he devoted his life to promotion of Dogra heritage sites and culture. He contributed for the Dogra interest at the following positions:

- As Board Member of Shri Mata Vaishno Devi Shrine Board for 7 years, involving himself in promoting this Dogra heritage site which is revered by millions of pilgrims every year
- As Member of the Advisory Board, J&K Dharmarth Trust promoting 125 heritage temples, most of which are at Jammu and also to contributing to the wellbeing of over 500 employees of the Trust, most of whom are Dogras
- As Vice President of Sarvodaya International Trust, he spread the Gandhian philosophy among Dogras and other locals besides helping the leprosy and blind children in Jammu
- As President, Forum for Awareness of National Security for 6 years sensitizing and guiding the locals on the security of Jammu (Dogra) region

Author's Contribution in Recent Years

During 2023-25, Shiv Kumar devoted more time in putting a brake to the decline of Dogra language. He took 3-pronged action in this regard, and these are:

- **At the Govt. level:** He prepared a detailed proposal for making Dogri language compulsory at the school level and physically interacted with the following govt officials:
  - Sh. Manoj Sinha, Lt. Governor UT of J&K
  - Sh. Rajiv Bhatnagar, Advisor to Lt. Governor, UT of J&K
  - Sh. Piyush Singla, Secretary to Govt, School Education Dept.
  - Sh. Rakesh Magotra, Project Director Samagra Shiksha, J&K
  - Prof. Parikshat Manhas, Chairman, Board of School Education and Director SCERT J&K
  - Sh. Jagdeep Padha, Chief Education Officer, Jammu
  - And Vice Chancellors of the three universities located at Jammu

All were convinced to introduce Dogri language at the school level in line with the requirement spelled out in NEP-2020 and also give impetus to it at the institution level. Prof. Sanjeev Jain, Vice Chancellor has even agreed to open a Centre for Takri Script at his university.

- **At the School level:** He went to around 20 schools and conducted Dogri Essay Competition. Also introduced the concept of celebration of Dogri Manyata Week from 16-22 December every year.

  It was nice to see around 500 schools celebrating that and conducting Dogri programmes every day from 16 to 22 December 2024.

- **At the College level**: Gave the concept of forming Dogri Cultural Clubs in colleges. One such club has already started at Model Institute of Engineering and Technology (Autonomous), Jammu. Other colleges are also preparing to open these. These clubs conduct various Dogri programmes for the Dogra students who have not studied Dogri language during their college times and this way remain in touch with their culture..

- **At the International/National levels**: He was instrumental in forming the DOGRA-Bangalore organization, interacting with Dogra Sabha, Chandigarh, Dogra organizations at Delhi, Noida and Bombay besides the Dogra/Jammu organizations in the U.K and USA. He has been in touch with them and is trying to form a common forum for all Dogra organizations outside Jammu and outside India.

- **Revival of Takri Script**: Original script of Dogri language is Takri which has now become extinct. To revive that script, he has submitted a proposal to the Central University of Jammu which has been approved in principle by the Vice Chancellor of the university. It is now likely to start its functioning after getting due funding from the higher authorities.

The services of Shiv Kumar Sharma have been recognized by the society, and they have bestowed awards on him during 2024. (refer Fig. 13.4 and 13.5)

Efforts for Reviving Takri Script

Takri was the original script for Dogri, and other Pahari languages like Chambeali, Jaunsari and Kulvi spoken in Jammu, Himachal Pradesh, some parts of Punjab and Uttarakhand. It is derived from the Sharda script, another ancient writing system of this region and was used between the 16th and 19th centuries extensively. However, this script started dying in the 20th century.

In 1944, it was decided by Dogri Sanstha that the official script for Dogri would be *Devnagri* and stopped using Takri. In Chamba State, it was the official language till 1948 after which Hindi took its place. So, it is almost extinct in most of the places.

Revival efforts first started in Kulu, H.P when in Feb 2006, a workshop to provide training in Takri script was conducted to write Kulvi language in Takri. In 2009, H.P govt. established a program in association with IGNOU to train specialists in Takri under guidance of the National Manuscripts Mission.

In Nov 2019, as part of UN International Year for Cultural Excellence, a Dogri poem written by Dogri poetess Heena Mahajan and transcribed into Takri script, was cited by Manu Khajuria, Founder of Voice of Dogras, at the House of Lords in London.

An organization, *Sambh,* based at Dharmsala, H.P has decided to develop fonts for this script.

H.P govt., under the National Manuscript Mission Yojana, has set up a Manuscript Resource Centre and so far 1.26 lakh manuscripts, including that of Takri, have been catalogued. They have also decided to digitize these.

In Jammu, Senior Citizens SS Club Chowadi has started making display boards in Takri and placing these at the prominent locations to promote Takri. Even the top bureaucrats and industrialists are being requested to give publicity to it. A few of the boards are given on Fig. 13.6

Apart from this, Dr. Shikha Magotra, a Ph.D in Computer Science with thesis in Takri from SMVDU Jammu, has taken the initiative to revive this language. During August 2023, she started an online course in Takri language named *Dogra Mittar*. Two batches have already completed this course. With the locals joining the further courses, the old Takri script is likely to get a big boost.

At the Central University of Jammu, the Linguistics Department is preparing a proposal for getting a grant for starting a "Centre for Reviving Takri script". Prof. Sanjeev Jain, Vice Chancellor of the University, is very confident of getting the grant from the University Grants Commission to start this Centre. Once this Centre is opened, then the revival of Takri will be faster.

At the international level, Takri script was added to the Unicode Standard in 2012. It appears that these efforts will revive an almost dead script.

Heritage Places of Dogras

Amar Mahal

Mubarik Mandi

Bhim Garh Fort, Reasi

Dogra Art Museum

Fig 13.1: Dogra heritage places

Dogra Culture Promotion Activities in Schools and Colleges

Pugri Tying Competition

Dogri Dress Competition

Release of Dogra Magazine

Dogri Essay Competition

Fig 13.2a: Dogra cultural activities and dress competition in schools and colleges

Fig 13.2b: Dogra dress promotion in society

Fig 13.3: Prominent personalities pursuing Dogra cause

Fig 13.4: Duggar Gourav Samman Award to Shiv Kumar, Co-author of the book from The American University USA in collaboration with UN University for Global Peace

Fig 13.5: Duggar Gourav Samman to Shiv Kumar, Co-author of the book from M/s Parmeshwari CCC Trust and PKS Films Creation

Fig 13.6: A few of the boards in Takri script at prominent places in Jammu city

Section IV:

TEMPLATE FOR REVIVING ENDANGERED GLOBAL CULTURES

DESIRED ROLE OF THE GOVERNMENT

*The care of human life and happiness, and not their destruction,
is the first and only object of good government."*

*– Thomas Jefferson,
3rd President of USA during 1801-1809*

Details of the endangered cultures and the languages have amply been covered in the previous chapters. Organizations at the global level like the UN, UNESCO etc. have taken steps and issued guidelines to save and preserve endangered languages, however finally it is up to the national governments who are to take steps to ensure that.

It is heartening to see that awareness in this regard is slowly and slowly percolating to many countries and they have started taking initiatives too. Still, many other countries have not taken any steps to preserve these endangered languages as they are not aware of the actions to be taken at their level. So, a template based on the methodology adopted for the successful revival of the Dogra Culture has been suggested for them to initiate the actions.

Why Dogra Template for Revival of Languages?

After studying many success stories of the cultures in the world which recovered from their decline path and got revived, it was inferred to adopt the template of the Dogra culture of India. This culture is one such culture that had been flourishing in the past but suddenly started moving on the path of decline. On sensing this, the government and civil society took some exemplary steps, stopped the decline, started moving ahead and is flourishing now.

In the erstwhile State of Jammu and Kashmir, India, Dogri was the official language of the state and the ruler of the state was Maharaja Hari Singh, a Dogra king. As per some reports the number of Dogri speaking people in 1941 was 10.75 Lakh., however a few other reports brought out that pure Dogri-speaking people were around 6.9 Lakhs and other 4 lakh was a mix of people from RS Pura, Miran Sahib and Sialkot areas who were Dogras but speaking Dogri as well as Punjabi languages. However, it can be safely assumed that the Dogri speaking population was between 8 to 9 lakhs in 1941.

On the merger of the state with the Indian Union in 1947, the Dogra king had to leave the state and was replaced by Sheikh Mohd. Abdullah, who was anti Dogras (as per Dr. Karan Singh, erstwhile Sadr-e-Riyasat of J&K). Dogri language lost its status and was neither given a place in the 14 national languages nor retained as the official language of the State of Jammu and Kashmir. This led to the commencement of the decline of Dogri language and the Dogra culture.

The next census which took place after 20 years in the State of Jammu & Kashmir in 1961, it was assumed that Dogra population would have gone up by 50-60% to around 13-15 lakh. However, when the actual counting took place, it was seen that the population of Dogri speaking people had reduced to 8.69. Had this trend of the last 20 years (1941-1961) continued, the Dogra population would have either vanished by now or fallen in the category of "Critically Endangered Languages". However, the steps taken by the government as well as the civil society brought it back to sound footing and the population rose to 26 lakhs in the census of 2011. Reasons for its decline have been covered in the last chapter along with the spectacular revival efforts made by the government as well as the social organizations.

The above facts bring out clearly that revival of the Dogra culture has been spectacular and that is the reason for recommending this template for all those cultures which are either in the list of endangered cultures or on the declining path.

During the revival of Dogra culture, the initiatives were taken at the levels of the government as well as the civil society. These initiatives are being covered in detail in this chapter along with the suggestions from the authors' side for successful revival of the cultures which are in the endangered list or likely to fall in that category soon.

Initiatives at the Government Level

Govt. can play a very important role in the revival of the cultures which are endangered in their region. Thereafter, it must include the following aspects as their key areas:

- **Legislation and Policy**: With the consensus of all the parties including representatives of the indigenous cultures, it should enact laws and make policies which would preserve the endangered languages. It involves recognizing and safeguarding the indigenous rights and heritage.
- **Education**: Integrate traditional culture into the curricula of schools and colleges thus creating awareness among the younger generations about the cultures of each region in the country. During the routine annual and biannual functions of the educational institutions, they should perform activities like poem recitation, plays, skits, songs etc. based on local traditions and cultures. Govt. should cater for additional funding for these activities.

- **Establish Cultural Institutions**: These are the cultural academies, museums, heritage sites, cultural artifacts centres, etc. These institutions should be made as hubs of all cultural activities in the region. Regions where endangered tribes stay should preferably be promoted by creating a tourist place around it, if possible.
- **Community Engagement**: Methods should be put in place to have active participation of all the stakeholders including the endangered communities. Senior citizens could also be involved as their knowledge of culture is more which they can pass on to others. Incentive schemes for community participation should be incorporated.
- **Internal Promotion and Awareness Campaign**: Periodic campaigns should be launched to showcase the old cultures of each tribe or endangered community.
- **Participation in International Organizations**: UNESCO has initiated many programmes for promoting cultures in the countries and issued guidelines. Governments must participate in all their programmes and follow the guidelines issued by them, as far as possible.
- **Funding**: Finally, the govt. should earmark sufficient funds to give grants and subsidies for all the above initiatives. It must be kept in mind that no success is achieved till proper financial provision is made in the budget. So, in the annual or 5-year plans, suitable budgetary provisions must be made for all these activities.
- **Compilation of Directory:** A directory of the cultures which are in the endangered list must be made. This directory can be compiled based on the decadal census of the country which would have taken place, maybe, during 2021. In case it is not done, then this list is to be prepared by the respective departments of the government, so that further action at various levels could be decided.

Department wise Role

The following departments of the government have a great role to play, and their action plan is also discussed below:

- Department of Education
- Department of Culture
- A special department for the tribes/indigenous people/aboriginal people (or whatever name they are called in a country)
- A General Administration Dept. to issue guidelines to all the depts. and govt. organizations

In case any dept. is not existing, then the duties of that dept. could be handed over to some other dept. or else an independent dept. could be opened in the govt. set up.

Department of Education

This dept. has a very vital role in the country. It must ensure that each of the languages gets a fair chance to grow in the country. For that, following steps are required to be taken:

a. **Issue National Education Policy Document**: It should frame a National Education Policy (NEP) spelling out the salient parameters for growth of all languages including those which are spoken by a very less number of people. An example of Govt. of India could be taken where this policy, called NEP-2020, was issued by that Government. Special features of the policy are:
   - Teaching of mother tongue is made compulsory for all the school going children up to Class 5th and preferably up to Class 8th.
   - Three-Language Formula was enforced. As per this, the first language to be taught is the mother tongue/native language, second is the regional language and third would be the national language.
   - The National Curriculum Framework (NCF) was prepared giving guidelines to all the regional headquarters, schools and other stakeholders the methodology to adopt the NEP.

b. **Establish a Centre of Indigenous Languages (CIL):** This Centre is required to identify the endangered languages, prepare documents in such a way that these could be preserved. Its detailed role could be under:

   o   To conduct research in the major areas of language analysis, language pedagogy, language technology and language use.

   o   The questionnaire be prepared to be filled in by the locals with the aim to get exact details of the languages and the culture like:

       ➢   the number of speakers of the language

       ➢   occupation and their economic conditions

       ➢   status of the original script of the language in case it had existed

       ➢   their festivals, customs, folk songs, folklore, traditions

       ➢   heritage buildings and assets

       ➢   their health parameters

       ➢   any difficulty faced by them in retaining their culture

       ➢   suggestions from their side to preserve and promote their culture

In India, the corresponding institution is CIIL (Central Institute for Indian Languages) which has launched a scheme named "Scheme for Protection and Preservation of Endangered Languages" under which the tasks mentioned above are undertaken. Besides this, technological help is taken to take pictures, record the audios and also prepare the academic literature for the school and college going students. Techniques like *artificial intelligence* and *natural language processing* are used to document all activities.

c. **Funding:** Allot suitable funds for all the activities, which must be enhanced periodically. Even some of the activities could be sponsored in collaboration with civil society.

d. **Calendar for Celebration of Cultural Days:** Issue instructions to educational institutions to celebrate the important days connected with the local culture so that the children know about their culture and also the children of other cultures become aware of others' cultures too. In the case of Dogra culture, following days were agreed to be celebrated:

- o **Dogri Manyata Week (16-22 December).** Dogri language was included in the 8th Schedule of the Indian Constitution thus giving it a national status on 22 Dec 2003. This recognition is celebrated the whole week by having activities like Dogri essay competition, Dogri dance competition, Dogri turban tying competition etc. During the morning assembly time, stories of Dogra culture are told to students, making everyone know about that culture. Some schools even show Dogri films to the students. So, any auspicious day, connected with the culture is declared and the complete week is celebrated.

- o **International Mother Tongue Day on 21st February:** This day has been declared by UNESCO and thus reminds all of us to have some cultural program on that day, thereby making everyone realize the importance of the mother tongue.

- o Festivals like *Lohri, Baisakhi, Bachh Dua* etc. that are related to Dogra culture must be celebrated in the schools.

Department of Culture

It is another important department which keeps a nation united by promoting cultural values of every community staying in that nation. The communities which are on the endangered list are given special care and programmes are launched to revitalize their languages, scripts, manuscripts, heritage sites etc. The Department of Culture in the State of Jammu and Kashmir, India, is a good example to follow. It has three verticals under it which perform the task of preserving the existing cultures.

- **Academy of Art, Culture and Languages**: This academy has taken on several roles for all the languages of each culture including the endangered cultures. It undertakes the following activities:
  - o Literature of each language is published. This literature is in the form of books on poems, novels and other topics.

- o A magazine is published periodically in which articles written by authors of various languages are published.
- o It offers a platform for creative expression to the young and budding writers, encourages writers achieve excellence and contributes seriously to develop their language by publishing translated literature of the sister languages.
- o It encourages research work related to the cultural heritage and history pertaining to each language.
- o It publishes anthologies and dictionaries of each language.
- o It collects manuscripts, rare documents, folk songs and folk tales.
- o It prints books of songs and folk tales in regional languages.

- **Directorate of Archives, Archaeology and Museums**: The Directorate takes on the role of identifying and preserving the rich cultural heritage of the State in different forms like archival records, archaeological monuments and antiquities. For this, it has established its museums and repositories at different central locations through its various establishments like Archival Repositories, Archaeology and State Museums. It undertakes the following activities:
  - o It conducts regular surveys, carries out identification and excavation of archaeological sites in order to include these sites/ monuments in the list of protected monuments of the country or state.
  - o It preserves its archival records and makes these available to scholars and historians for their research work.
  - o For safety and security of old records, proper scientific and chemical treatment is given to these.
  - o The records are also digitized so that easy access is provided to the scholars who need these, and permanent safety of the record is ensured.
  - o To showcase the heritage of various cultures, it maintains separate enclosures of artifacts and antiquities in the museums.
  - o The quantity of artifacts is enhanced by different means like excavations, donations and purchase.

- **Directorate of Libraries and Research:** This department has established a network of libraries at district, tehsil and block levels where free library and reading room facilities are provided to the public. Books with various titles and newspapers are kept for the readers. Books are provided for each section of society like children, senior citizens, scholars and people belonging to endangered cultures. Even manuscripts and rare books are also provided. Besides the above, it performs the following duties:
  - Holds seminars, debates, book exhibitions to generate awareness about the written records
  - Promotes local languages by purchasing books from local authors
  - Publishes manuscripts in form of books
  - Undertakes the task of digitization and archival of the manuscripts and rare/reference books

They believe in the saying of Jason Thomson that:

"Books are more than pages, board, glue and thread- they are artifacts of the human spirit and hand. "

Department of Tribal Affairs / Indigenous People / Aboriginal people

In case the population or the number of endangered cultures is large in number, then it would be worthwhile having a separate ministry for them in the government. This would specifically look after their issues thus promoting each culture. They can start with the following initiatives for each of the endangered cultures or tribes:

- Ensure social security for the community
- Make arrangements for the hostel facilities for the children who want to attain higher education in other cities
- Provide in-situ vocational training to the members thus improving their employability chances
- Planning for scholarships/awards for those students who work for their community or the tribe.

- Promote social and economic empowerment for them so that they can live a dignified life.
- Provide institutional support for the development of local produce and help them market the same in an effective manner with greater reach.

Other Government Departments

It is the duty of every department in the government to keep in mind the cultures which are dwindling in society and make plans to push these up to avoid their premature death. A few of the salient actions to be taken by various other departments in the govt, to preserve and promote each culture, are explained below.

- **Details of each Culture**: Each dept must have a list of the cultures which are endangered and where special care is to be taken.
- **Generate in-situ Employment Opportunities**: By creating employment opportunities for the endangered cultures in their own area and also establishing systems so that the local culture gets promoted. A few of the methods are as under:
  - Promote that area as a tourist spot as has been done by the US government for Amish culture in Pennsylvania, USA
  - Establish some good industries like a hospital, university or an industry to produce items using local resources available where the endangered community stays. This will generate employment, and the locals would then prefer to stay at their place helping preserve culture. Example can be taken of the Dogra community at village Painthal, J&K, India who were moving to better places for jobs thus thinning the population of that village. But the government. planned SMVD Narayana Super Specialty Hospital, SMVD University and a few institutions at that location. These organizations generated livelihood for the locals. They stopped moving out of their villages thus helping restore the culture there itself.

- Get involved in the cultural events, arrange or provide sponsorships for organizing events at those places.
- Provide financial help to the people belonging to those cultures.

This way if all the departments of the govt. keep trying from their side and give boost to endangered cultures, these are sure to revive.

Fig. 14.1: Websites of the government departments preserving and promoting culture in the State of J&K

Fig. 14.2: Establishments opened up in a village *Panthal* to stop migration of local villagers to other locations for search of jobs thus stabilizing the population there.

Chapter 15

DESIRED ACTIONS BY CIVIL SOCIETY

"Generations have struggled to learn, despite efforts to eliminate our traditions and language. Having a strong sense of yourself
and your community is a great foundation for learning."

- Agnes Chavis
NC Association of Educators, NC, USA

Details of the endangered cultures and the languages have amply been covered in the previous chapters. Organizations at the global level like the UN, UNESCO etc. have taken steps and issued guidelines to save and preserve the endangered languages, however, finally it is up to the national governments who are to take steps to ensure that.

It is heartening to see that awareness in this regard is slowly and slowly percolating in many countries and they have started taking initiatives too. Actions taken by some prominent countries have also been covered in earlier chapters. Still, many countries have not yet taken any step to preserve these endangered languages as they themselves are not aware of the actions to be taken at their level. So, a template for them may assist in initiating the actions.

After studying many success stories, it is found that the template set by the revival of the Dogra culture in India is a good example, some aspects of which could be followed by the social organizations so that the endangered cultures do not die due to modernization or neglect by the government.

A few of the actions taken by the Dogra society which could be thought of as the turning point in the revival of Dogra culture are given here, just to give an idea that even when the government is against the endangered culture, how to force them and help save your culture.

Late Pandit Khem Chand (1915-2005), a philanthropist, who has seen the government of Dogra Maharajas in Jammu and Kashmir, India, for 32 years, could smell the disaster coming ahead for the Dogra culture after the new government under Mohd. Sheikh Abdullah took over in 1948. Jammu started losing its importance and the culture of the dominant Kashmir region started percolating in the Jammu region too. His voice still resonates in our heads:

"If the Dogra community does not wake up now, agitate and force the new government to respect and honour the dignity of the Dogras, this culture would not last long."

Soon the community woke up, and in association with other organizations, launched a massive agitation called *The Praja Parishad Agitation of 1952-53*. Mr. BD Sharma, IAS, a senior bureaucrat who served the Jammu and Kashmir government for over 30 years, in an article in the prominent newspaper *Daily Excelsior*, gave an account of this agitation. Had the Dogra community not woken up and gone for that agitation, the Dogra community would have become extinct by now. Extracts from his article are reproduced below:

"With the departure of Maharaja and the policies framed by the new set up, made the people of Jammu suspicious of the intentions of the new government. He (Sheikh Mohd. Abdullah) had pushed his agenda of "Naya Kashmir" ignoring the aspirations of the Jammuites. He didn't stop at that only and even brought around Nehru, the Prime Minister of India, to rechristen the State as "Kashmir State" despite the fact that it was known as the State of Jammu and Kashmir right from 1846. Name of the

State was mentioned as "Kashmir" in the Schedule of States in the draft Constitution of India. The Sheikh did not succeed in this venture, however, succeeded in another game plan when he got the constituencies for the Constituent Assembly of the State delineated in such a way that Kashmir Valley took away the lion's share. The Jammu region was left with thirty segments out of the seventy-five despite the population ratio of 45:55. He inducted only one minister from Jammu in the State Cabinet of five. In this way, the crafty Sheikh ensured that Jammu didn't get rightful, inspiring and distinguished representation in the power structure. All these developments instilled a sense of fear and anxiety in the minds of Jammu people."

Quite agitated, the Jammu Dogras formed a political party *Praja Parishad,* and started channeling the resentment of the people. It joined hands with other existing parties, took their agenda points too and started framing the agitation plan. The activities that followed are proof of this.

- Student agitation was launched in GGM Science College, Jammu when the flag of Kashmir-based party National Conference was hoisted at a function.
- *Lok Satyagraha* started on 14th November 1952 and their leader Pandit Prem Nath Dogra was arrested.
- People in Udhampur agitated and in police firing 300 people got injured.
- On the 11th of January 1953, a massive demonstration of 5000 persons was fired upon killing two persons and injuring more than 70 at Hiranagar. Similar demonstrations took place in other places like Jourian, Ramban etc.,
- Took the help of national parties like Hindu Mahasabha, Akali Dal, Jan Sangh who gave a nationwide call for strike on 5th March 1953.

The aim of bringing out the above events is that sometimes, the civil society has to agitate, take strong actions, and even give sacrifices in case the government is against them. That is the way of making the culture survive.

The number of Dogri knowing people which were around 1 million in 1941 had reduced to just 800 thousand by 1961. But with the actions taken by civil society, it forced the govt. to take positive steps, which led the population of Dogras to surge again and as per the last Census of 2011, their population was 2.6 million.

Actions taken by Dogra society are a good example for societies of other cultures which are in the endangered list. Salient actions suggested for civil society are explained here.

Formation of Central Organization

In the case of Dogra culture, some of the prominent organizations were already existing in the society before its decline started. These organizations are Dogra Sadar Sabha formed by Maharaja Partap Singh, Raja Amar Singh and other stalwarts of the Dogras in 1904 and Dogri Sanstha, formed in 1944. Later, many region-based organizations also took birth to promote the cause of the local culture.

Hence, there is a need to have an organization which could promote the cause of the endangered cultures. The composition of the Management Committee of this central organization should have the following members:

- **Head of the Organization**: An elderly individual who is respected the most in the community, has convincing power, is passionate for his culture and is a selfless worker with organizing capabilities.
- **General Secretary**: Comparatively a younger individual who has a good wicket with the Head of the organization, is energetic and can muster people for the organization.
- **Other Members**: They should be from different backgrounds like an educated individual (a think tank) who is connected to the outside world, a financier who can muster funds, a planner who has a long-term vision for the community etc.

Actions by the Management Committee

The committee must decide to have periodic meetings, see the on-ground situation and press on the government to take actions for the safety and preservation of their culture. Their first step should be to collect the following data about their society before making any plan:

- Total number of people in the community/tribe
- Number of people (population) in the last census or around 10-20 years ago
- In case these have decreased over years, then the reasons for the same.
- Do the school-going children avoid following their own culture and attracted to other dominant languages?
- Any discrimination faced by them from other powerful/dominating cultures or outside settlers
- Reasons for their economic backwardness
- The standard of health, education, earning capability etc. of the locals
- Are the guidelines of the international organizations like the UNO, UNESCO etc. regarding endangered communities being followed by the government? These guidelines included celebration of *the International Year of the Indigenous Languages - 2019*, *Decade for the International Languages, 2022-2032* etc.

Preparation for Futuristic Plan

After collecting all the data, one is clear about the action to be taken by the committee. The think tank in the team can make long-term as well as short-term plans. The components of the plan could be as below:

- Together, we need to force the government on certain issues. These could be:
  - Opening a Ministry of Culture or Ministry of Tribal Affairs etc.
  - Start industries in the tribal areas so that they do not have to move out of their territories to start earning

- Develop tourist spots in their areas so that the tourism industry helps in their livelihood
- Have an educational policy which promotes education of the tribal culture among the children.
- Make a calendar of cultural events so that each culture showcases itself and children learn from them
- Have income generating system for the religious preachers in the tribe
- Heritage places be preserved and due funds be kept for those.
- System of giving incentives to the students who showcase their culture
- Have monitoring systems in place to see progress

- Actions to be taken on the ground level to muster support of maximum members in the community in case the government does not pay heed to their peaceful demands.
- Need to educate children and take them on board. In case no policy is made by the government then the elderly people in the community must go to schools and make a system of educating the students and other children
- Policies to be made by the government for the children as well as action by the local community members to inculcate community culture in them
- Relay of cultural programmes on local television, radio and other media channels.

Formation of Activity Based Teams

To pursue each activity of the culture, dedicated teams are required to be constituted. If need is felt, then, a few of the activities could also be clubbed under one team. These teams are as below:

- **Script Promotion Team**: A unique script of a language is the identity of that culture. This team will promote the spread of the script among their children and society. They should encourage the writers to produce interesting literature in that script. In some cultures, it is observed that either the script has become extinct or the culture has adopted some other dominant script for continuing literary work.

In the case of Dogri language, the original script was Takri, which has now become almost extinct. So, the cultural organizations adopted *Devnagri* as their script to keep generating literature for the society.

- **Language Promotion Teams:** There could be teams or sub teams to take on each aspect of language promotion. At least the following two teams must be formed as far possible:
  - Team A: This team should take the responsibility of motivating the elder generations to enthuse cultural sentiments in their children, talk to them in their native language at residences and tell them stories of the role models of their tribes/cultural societies. Also encourage them to read books written in their native languages.
  - Team B: This team should promote the writers, teaching fraternity, senior citizens and senior students to write books, novels, plays etc. in that language. Even the translation work of good books of other cultures should be undertaken to increase the treasure of literature. They should also motivate the influential people of their tribe to institute some awards for those who write good literature. Even the liaison should be made with the government departments to get some awards instituted by them for the best books of this language. This will encourage more writers to produce good literature.

In case of Dogri language, it was included for the Sahitya Academy Awards as a separate language in 1969, and Narendra Khajuria was the first recipient of this award for Dogri language in 1970. It encouraged many people to write in Dogri. As on date there are awards in many categories like poetry, novels, short stories, plays, essays, literary criticism etc. Even the award for translation of good works has been instituted. Besides, to encourage children and young people, the awards like Bal Sahitya Puraskar, Yuva Puraskar etc. have been included. This has encouraged many Dogras to switch to writing in their native language and get recognized.

- **Dress Promotion Team**: Every community has its own traditional dress. Though these days people have switched to the common dress code consisting of a simple shirt and trousers, still they use their traditional dress on specific occasions. There is a need to make it more frequent and the natives should continue wearing it during festivals, fairs, marriages, rituals and gatherings. With a unique dress, one is recognized even from a far-off distance.

In Jammu, Prof. Kul Bhushan Mohtra, MD Parmeshwari CCC Trust, launched a campaign of wearing *Safaa* (a different type of turban) at least once a week. One can now find that the Dogras have started feeling proud by wearing it on different occasions. This campaign is still continuing. Figs. 15.1 and 15.2 give a glimpse of these activities started among the students of Jammu.

- **Role Model Promotion Team**: This team should identify the role models of their culture. They could be warriors, sports persons, selfless social workers, those who rose to national and international levels and the ones who sacrificed their lives for the sake of saving their culture. Stories of these role models motivate children and all in the society and may encourage one to feel proud as part of that culture.

Birthdays, death anniversaries, or other significant days attached with them must be identified and a message should be spread to all to celebrate these wherever possible. A calendar of these activities be prepared and made available to most of the cultural institutions.

- **Cultural Events Promotion Team**: This team must be in search of the days and duration when cultural events could be celebrated. All the schools, colleges, and other organizations, including government ones, should be made aware of these for celebration. Also, at least two or three cultural events to be selected and declared as important, so that everyone is motivated to celebrate these at least once or twice in a year.

This team should also identify the heritage places and find ways so that the school and college students visit these periodically. Liaison should be made with the govt. agencies to get a few of these included in the national or UNESCO heritage list so that these become tourist attractions which would increase the income of that place and livelihood of the locals.

- **Media Team**: Spreading awareness about the culture and motivating all for adhering to the cultural values, this team must utilize the print as well as the electronic media techniques.

So, if civil society participates actively, even the dying cultures would get revived soon and one will feel proud and a lucky member of that particular culture.

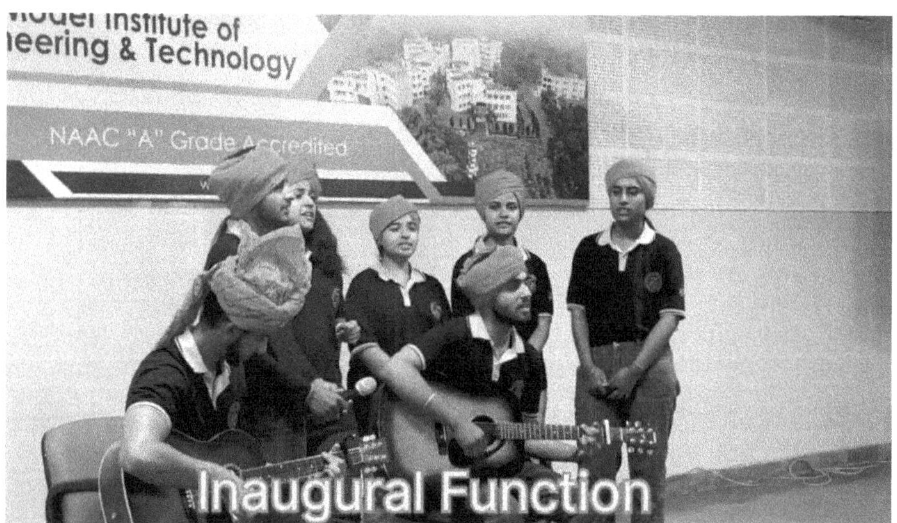

Fig 15.1: Promoting wearing of Turban among college students as identity of Dogra culture

(Source: MIET Dogra Cultural Club, Jammu, India)

Fig 15.2: Promoting wearing of traditional dress among school students as identity of Dogra culture

(Source: Senior Citizens SS Club, Chowadi, Jammu, India)

Fig 15.3: Boards in 4 scripts including Takri, the almost extinct script of Dogri language, have recently been found in front of many organizations in Jammu city, as part of Takri script revival drive

CONCLUSION

This book attempts to highlight the importance of each culture, however small it may be. Main focus was on the cultures which have been declared endangered by the UNESCO.

If one looks around the globe, one will observe that national governments of all countries are spending millions and billions of dollars to learn about the past, undertake excavations, preserve the excavated sites etc. There are full-fledged departments in the governments, with huge budgets, designed to study the past and preserve it in case they find any artefacts.

In USA, the annual budget for the year 2025 for the Department of Archeology and Historical Preservation is $13.6 million. Besides this, many connected departments also, spend money on the same or similar tasks. The Department of Anthropology is found in almost all the major universities of the USA which keep substantial budgets for this activity.

In India, a whopping amount of Rs. 1,274 crore (around $146 million) has been catered for the Department of Archaeological Survey of India for the year 2024-25.

A commonsense question bothers our minds that the governments spend a lot of money on cultures which are no longer now and have become extinct. We do excavations and start learning as to how the people in those days used to stay. But we do not bother about the cultures which are still existing and are in the endangered list. If these are not saved, these may also become extinct in decades to come. And then we'll spend money to know how they were staying at that time. It appears foolish sometimes.

We, as authors, have tried our best to sensitize everyone through this book the urgent need to preserve all the endangered cultures. After studying many success stories, we have suggested the methodology adopted by the once flourishing Dogra society to revive their culture which had already started moving down the hill.

It is our earnest wish that the governments and civil society take cue from here and ensure that the endangered cultures in their areas do not die down but survive and flourish. We can assure you of the immense enjoyment you would get by doing this action.

Wishing all a happy reading!